Dmitri Shostakovich: A Life in Film

KINOfiles Filmmakers' Companions
General Editor: Richard Taylor

Written for cineastes and students alike, and building on the achievements of the KINOfiles Film Companions, the KINOfiles Filmmakers' Companions are readable, authoritative, illustrated companion handbooks to the most important and interesting people who have participated in Russian cinema from its beginnings to the present. Each KINOfile examines the career of one filmmaker, or group of filmmakers, in the context of both Russian and world cinema. KINOfiles also include studies of people who have been active in the cinemas of the other countries that once formed part of the Soviet Union, as well as of émigré filmmakers working in the Russian tradition.

KINOfiles form a part of KINO: The Russian Cinema Series.

Filmmakers' Companions:

1	*Nikita Mikhalkov*	Birgit Beumers
2	*Alexander Medvedkin*	Emma Widdis
3	*Dmitri Shostakovich*	John Riley
4	*Kira Muratova*	Jane A. Taubman

Film Companions:

1	*The Battleship Potemkin*	Richard Taylor
2	*The Man with the Movie Camera*	Graham Roberts
3	*Burnt by the Sun*	Birgit Beumers
4	*Repentance*	Denise Youngblood and Josephine Woll
5	*Bed and Sofa*	Julian Graffy
6	*Mirror*	Natasha Synessios
7	*The Cranes Are Flying*	Josephine Woll
8	*Little Vera*	Frank Beardow
9	*Ivan the Terrible*	Joan Neuberger
10	*The End of St. Petersburg*	Vance Kepley, Jr.
11	*Chapaev*	Julian Graffy
12	*Storm over Asia*	Amy Sargeant

DMITRI SHOSTAKOVICH: A LIFE IN FILM

JOHN RILEY

KINOfiles Filmmakers' Companion 3

Published in 2005 by I.B.Tauris & Co. Ltd
6 Salem Road, London W2 4BU
175 Fifth Avenue, New York NY 10010
ibtauris.com

Copyright © John Riley, 2005

The right of the author of this work to be identified has been asserted by him in accordance with the Copyright, Designs and Patents Act 1988.

All rights reserved. Except for brief quotations in a review, this book, or any part thereof, may not be reproduced, stored in or introduced into a retrieval system, or transmitted, in any form or by any means, electronic, mechanical, photocopying, recording or otherwise, without the prior written permission of the publisher.

Hardback ISBN 1 85043 709 2
          EAN 978 1 85043 709 3
Paperback ISBN 1 85043 484 0
          EAN: 978 1 85043 484 9

A full CIP record for this book is available from the British Library

Typeset in Calisto by Dexter Haven Associates Ltd, London

Contents

List of Illustrations	vi
Preface	vii
Acknowledgements	viii
Note on Transliteration	ix
Introduction: 1906–1928, Early Life and Works	1
1 Beware of Music (1929–1933): *Poor Columbus* to *The Counterplan*	6
2 Intelligible to the Millions (1934–1939): *Ankara – Heart of Turkey* to *The Great Citizen*	22
3 Interlude (1939–1942): *The Silly Little Mouse* to *The Adventures of Korzinkina*	47
4 War and Cold War (1943–1953): *Zoya* to the Death of Stalin	51
5 An Uncertain Thaw (1954–1962): *The Song of the Rivers* to *Cheremushki*	77
6 Endgame (1964–1975): *Hamlet* to *King Lear*	94
7 Legacy	108
Notes	113
Curriculum Vitae	129
Filmography	141
Further Reading	149

List of Illustrations

1	*Sovetskii ekran*: Shostakovich's thoughts on cinema in 1929	8
2	*New Babylon*: the empty restaurant under threat from the Prussians	9
3	*Alone*: 'How Good Life Will Be!' – An ironic comment on life in the Altai	13
4	*The Golden Mountains*: the press book, featuring Shostakovich's music (courtesy of BFI Special Collections)	16
5	*The Counterplan*: all problems are resolved by returning to work	19
6	*Love and Hate*: despair at the treatment meted out by the Whites	24
7	*The Youth of Maxim*: the midnight sleigh ride	27
8	*The Vyborg Side*: Maxim leads the assault on the wine cellars	44
9	*Zoya*: Zoya's pursuer vents his frustration	53
10	*Pirogov*: a malevolent audience enjoys Pirogov's failed demonstration	61
11	*The Fall of Berlin*: 'Glory to the Great Stalin', reads the banner; 'Glory to Stalin,' sings the choir	69
12	*The Unforgettable Year 1919*: Rachmaninovian music leads the troops into battle	74
13	*The Gadfly*: music shows Arthur the malignancy of religion	81
14	*Cheremushki*: 'I live all alone, always alone, like dry land surrounded by water' – A momentary sadness	91
15	*King Lear*: the *yurodivy*, with the last (musical) word	106

Preface

Space does not permit me to discuss each of the hundreds of film cues that Shostakovich wrote (and not every one warrants comment), but all of his original film scores are included, with comments on the political and personal circumstances surrounding each one, and an analysis of the major cues. Also included are some films that use his music and some projects that he was to work on but, for whatever reason, did not.

> A barbarian-artist with a drowsy brush
> Daubs black over a genius painting
> And his anarchic drawing
> Senselessly scribbles over it.
>
> But over time the foreign paints
> Fall away like rotten scales;
> The genius painting reappears
> In its former beauty.
>
> Thus the delusions vanish
> From my exhausted soul
> And in their place arise
> Visions of original, pure days.
>
> Pushkin (1819)/Shostakovich (1936/7)

Acknowledgements

My first thanks must go to Richard Taylor, Julian Graffy, Birgit Beumers, Emmanuel Utwiller of the Centre Chostakovitch in Paris and all at I.B.Tauris.

Thanks to Duncan Petrie and Colin MacCabe, the book's kernel began under the auspices of the BFI staff research scheme. Beyond that, the friends, relations, colleagues and acquaintances listed below provided (knowingly or not) information, translations, conversations, invitations, suggestions and digressions, as well as material, practical, physical and spiritual help and advice. Colleagues at the British Universities Film and Video Council, and former colleagues at the British Film Institute (BFI), Kenzo Amoh, Sergio Angelini, Neil Edmunds, David Fanning, Mark Fitz-Gerald, Stanley Forman, Derek Hulme, Paul Ingram, Alexander Ivashkin, Edward Johnson, Emma Kerr (Boosey and Hawkes), Peter Lundin, Gerard McBurney, Alan Mercer (editor of *DSCH*), Michael Mishra, Janet Moat, Natalia Noussinova, Marianne Open, Saffron Parker, Anthony Phillips, Richard Pleak, David Pountney, Sylvie Pras, Marek Pytel, Sheldon Rich, David Riley, W. Mark Roberts, Pilar Rodas, Irina Antonova Shostakovich, Maxim Dmitrievich Shostakovich, Per Skans, all at the Society for Cooperation in Russian and Soviet Studies, Jane Taubman, Fiona Waller, Karen Wellen, John White, Josephine Woll, Andrew Youdell.

Needless to say the mistakes are mine. I hope I have remembered everyone and that there will be another edition to allow me to correct any oversights.

Special thanks go to Melissa. The book came together at a difficult moment in my life, and her support and understanding allowed me to continue. It is to her that I dedicate it.

John Riley

Note on Transliteration

Transliteration from the Cyrillic to the Latin alphabet is a perennial problem for writers on Russian subjects. I have opted for a dual system. In the text I have used the Library of Congress system (without diacritics), but I have broken away from this system (a) when a Russian name has a clear English version (e.g. Maria instead of Mariia, Alexander instead of Aleksandr); (b) when a Russian name has an accepted English spelling, or when Russian names are of Germanic origin (e.g. Meyerhold instead of Meierkhol'd; Eisenstein instead of Eizenshtein); (c) when a Russian name ends in –ii or –yi, this is replaced by a single –y (e.g. Dostoevsky) for a surname and a single –i for a first name (e.g. Grigori, Sergei). In the scholarly apparatus I have adhered to the Library of Congress system (with diacritics) for the specialist.

Introduction:
1906–1928, Early Life and Works

Dmitri Dmitrievich Shostakovich was born on 25 September 1906 in St Petersburg, and proved a precocious musician. He started composing when he was about ten, with an opera, a ballet and descriptive piano and orchestral pieces showing a leaning towards dramatic music. The first thing he preserved (an orchestral scherzo) was written when he was thirteen, and he completed his last work (the Viola Sonata) four days before his death fifty-six years later on 9 August 1975. In between he wrote symphonies and string quartets (fifteen of each), concertos and chamber, instrumental and vocal music. He also completed three ballets, two operas (and planned or started several others), an operetta and incidental music for the theatre, confirming his preference for the dramatic.

There is one other genre to which he made a significant contribution: film music. As a student he worked as a cinema pianist, and between 1929 and 1970 he wrote almost forty film scores, yet this work is generally overlooked.[1] Music critics often base their purely musicological judgements on the concert suites rather than the music as it appears in the films, seemingly unaware that film music and concert music have different criteria, though no opera critic ignores plot and characterisation. Meanwhile, film critics often seem oblivious to the soundtrack. Overlying this has been an opinion that the films themselves are 'mere propaganda' and thus beneath study. Finally, the difficulty in actually seeing many of them has made it easier to dismiss the work. As Soviet history and culture are reassessed, and film music's popularity increases, this is a good moment to re-examine this substantial part of his output. Not all are great films or great scores, but ignoring them leaves our understanding of him incomplete. The legendary Leninism that cinema was 'of all the arts, for us the most important'[2] was rooted in the medium's political potential, and even outside his cinema work Shostakovich was quickly primed as one of the first successes and vindications of the Soviet regime: his usefulness to the state was the prism through which his whole career was viewed, in both East and West. There is no greater proof than the argument that has raged around the book *Testimony*.[3] Presented as his memoirs, its protagonist is not a committed communist but a secret dissident whose music was an Aesopian attack on the Soviet state, though this blinded some to the book's attacks on the West. However, interpolations from older material threw doubt on whether it was what it claimed to be, opening another flank concentrating on the book as a fraud, irrespective of the accuracy of the portrait it painted.[4] Though its general tenor (and especially the idea of his working from behind a mask) is increasingly (though not universally) accepted, the longevity and ferocity of the debate is symptomatic of both sides' desire to claim Shostakovich as evidence in a political/aesthetic argument.

*   *   *

In 1922 Shostakovich's father died, impoverishing the family and aggravating Dmitri's tuberculosis. After recuperating in the Crimea he returned to Petrograd as a postgraduate, aiming to help the family's finances by giving concerts but, despite his mother's disapproval, ended up working as a cinema pianist. Cinema accompaniment at the time was of very variable quality, often relying on the ingenuity and resources of individual cinemas. These ranged from solo pianists to large orchestras, though the effectiveness of the latter was occasionally compromised by their habit of simply playing complete pieces of classical music (Tchaikovsky symphonies were favourites) regardless of the action on-screen.[5] In an effort to improve things the art workers' union introduced an exam, and Shostakovich sat his in 1923.

> First I was asked to play a 'blue waltz' and then 'something oriental'. At Bruni's [a former music teacher] I had not been able to play in the Eastern style, but by 1923 I knew Rimsky-Korsakov's *Scheherezade* and Cui's *Orientale*. I passed the test and in November started work at the Svetlaia lenta [Bright Reel] cinema.[6]

With his dramatic talent Shostakovich excelled at the work, and he soon became well known for it.[7] Despite the long hours – three shows per day – he thought it would be easier than giving concerts, which left him nervous beforehand and exhausted afterwards, and he hoped his mother would give up working as a cashier.[8] His letters of the time constantly mention the family's poverty so, whatever his political outlook, he chose the remnants of the private sector for its better conditions and higher wages, though on one occasion he had to sue for them, after being told that 'an art lover should not expect payment'.[9] Neither was it good for his health; some cinemas were cold at the start of the evening but fetid by the end, and he would walk home to save money, arriving after 1 a.m.[10] Given the industry's problems, many films were imported, and, being popular, raised valuable revenue but proving controversial. Pickford, Fairbanks and Chaplin were the biggest stars, but *Komsomolskaia pravda* railed against adopting bourgeois fashions under their corrosive influence, though this was already being reduced by re-editing.

Shostakovich began by enjoying the work – he once laughed so hard at a comedy that he had to stop playing, and was sacked[11] – but it soon became a chore; 'it takes up every evening and mechanically reproducing "human passions" on the piano is exhausting',[12] 'completely paralysing' his musical pursuits.[13] Each time he saved enough money he left, though several times he had to return. Late 1925 was a particularly difficult period, and he seems to have been under instruction as to the music he should play. In October he wrote to music theorist Boris Yavorsky:

> Now they are showing a drama, *The Great and the Eternal* [an as yet unidentified film]. It has been on without a break for five weeks. There is a full house every day and each time the music is the same. I am sick and tired of it.[14]

In November he wrote to his piano teacher, Leonid Nikolaev:

> I'm in a fix because of my cinema work. I may be too impressionable but when I come home the music rings in my ears and the hateful film characters keep me awake until 4 or 5. I wake up with a headache and in a bad mood. Ugly thoughts force themselves into my mind – I've sold myself to the Northwest Film Studios for 134 rubles. Then I have to hurry to the conservatory. Then I come home, have a quick meal and return to the Splendid palas [cinema]. Hopefully this will soon be over and I'll be able to study serious piano playing again.[15]

The pain must have been ameliorated by the salary (about a third more than the average worker's), but, apart from the money and piano practice, he used the work to develop his compositions; the First Symphony, with its concertante piano part and filmic structure, was a beneficiary. He finally left the work in March 1926, after the symphony had been accepted for publication and before its triumphant premiere on 12 May. In July the Association of Revolutionary Cinematography (ARK) began a 're-registration' (i.e. a purge), removing 40 per cent of its members, and in May 1927 sixteen cinema workers were imprisoned for misuse of advances.[16] Later that year Trotsky was exiled, confirming Stalin's grip, and in March 1928 the Party Conference on Cinema ordered films that were 'intelligible to the millions', a phrase that would echo down the years.[17] Meanwhile, Shostakovich was working on his Gogolian opera *The Nose*, which – though he did not know it – would lead to his return to the film industry at this, one of its most tumultuous moments.

* * *

'Silent cinema' is a misnomer: from the beginning the images were accompanied by live music or sound effects. Though Russia had been slow off the mark in developing a national industry, the first Russian fiction film, *Stenka Razin* [1908], had a score by the respected composer Mikhail Ippolitov-Ivanov. Based on the famous folk song, it showed how music could be used simplistically to tap into people's emotions; as Noel Coward observed: 'Strange, the potency of cheap music.' But major composers were not tempted into the new medium (even then, the apparent transience of film music was possibly a deterrent), and the few specially written scores were mostly by now-forgotten names.

Early film music was plagued by the simplistic literalism that Ippolitov-Ivanov displayed, and this was sometimes encouraged by directors, who were moving towards auteurist complete control. The very titles of Iakov Protazanov's films *A Chopin Nocturne* [Noktiurn Shopena, 1913] and *Moment musical* [Muzykal'nyi moment, 1913] instruct musicians as to what to play (in the latter case, a piece by Schubert). On a smaller scale, directors would sometimes include shots of sheet music to point the players in the right direction. Meanwhile, distributors were beginning to send out cue sheets that included themes with explanatory titles such as 'chase' or 'reverie' to spur musicians' imaginations. This was done partially to control the films' presentation and partially to generate more income. Some of Shostakovich's film scores use just such titles, but if he was presented with such cue sheets during his time in the pit he would probably have tried to ignore them, preferring to rely on his own musicality.

But some directors were beginning to think about the relationship between image and music in different ways, especially after the launching of synchronised sound in the West in the late 1920s. Just as with the initial development of its cinema industry, though, the Soviet Union again lagged behind. Nevertheless, the debate about how sound should be used entered a new phase. In their *Statement on Sound*, Eisenstein, Pudovkin and Alexandrov opposed realistic sound, proposing a 'counterpoint' between it and the image: 'The first experiments in sound must aim at a sharp discord with the visual images.'[18] Musical counterpoint comprises two or more *interdependent* voices, but here the image was the primary element, with the soundtrack either reflecting or setting up a 'sharp contrast' to it.

The *Statement*, published in 1928, was probably inspired by Eisenstein's experiences on his two most recent films. The literalist musical arranger for *October* [Oktiabr, 1927], seeing a bridge being raised that left a horse hanging over the side, immediately suggested 'The Ride of the Valkyries', while Leonid Sabaneyev pronounced the maggoty meat in *The Battleship Potemkin* [Bronenosets Potemkin, 1926] 'unworthy of music'.[19] When it was premiered at the Bolshoi Theatre, the orchestra played a pot-pourri of classics, including Litolff's *Robespierre* Overture, Beethoven's *Egmont* Overture and Tchaikovsky's

Francesca da Rimini. To create the radical scores Eisenstein had in mind it was left to Edmund Meisel for the films' releases in Germany, and these, though written by an Austrian, are – ironically – among the best-known Soviet silent film scores.[20]

One of the most radical solutions was Dziga Vertov's 'score' for his own *The Man with a Movie Camera* [Chelovek s kinoapparatom, 1929]. Vertov provides general directions, leaving the details to the players ('a universally familiar intimate melody; piano and violin') and sometimes moves closer to noise ('persistent muffled hammering like the beat of a march, staccato low pitch').[21] But popular films, seen as less important in proving the regime's progressive credentials, were allowed more populist scores, and it is interesting to consider whether, had they had such music, the avant-garde classics would have proved more popular, if artistically compromised.

* * *

Shostakovich probably knew Eisenstein's circle through his friend the theatre director Vsevolod Meyerhold and would have taken an interest in these experiments, but his first cinema work was with FEKS (the Factory of the Eccentric Actor), led by Leonid Trauberg, Grigori Kozintsev, Sergei Yutkevich and Georgi Kryzhitsky. Their manifesto,[22] published in 'Eccentropolis (formerly Petrograd)', 'flings the galoshes of prosperity and good taste into the faces of the deserving': the old, the established, technophobes and haters of demotic art, such as the circus.[23] Out-*épatering* the Futurists, they parodied the title of Mayakovsky's famous poem *A Cloud in Trousers* with their headline 'Salvation in the Trousers', saw art in 'the shouts of newspaper-sellers, scandals, policemen's truncheons, noise, shouting, stamping, running', and preferred a 'Pinkerton cover [popular American detective fiction] to the concoction of Picasso' – 'Americanisation' was central to FEKS. Their 1922 staging of Gogol's *The Marriage* (subtitled *A Gag in Three Acts*) included clips of Chaplin films,[24] and its poster punned on Lenin's description of communism as 'Soviet power plus the electrification of the entire country' by promising 'the electrification of Gogol'. Shostakovich shared their enthusiasm for the Russian author and the American star, making him the ideal composer for their new film about the Paris Commune, *New Babylon* [Novyi Vavilon, 1929], and, as he had been so offended by cliché in the cinema pit, he accepted this opportunity to write an original score. But Eccentrism's 'defamiliarisation', which tried to subvert automatic responses and render the everyday strange, was too closely related to Formalism, later the most serious charge that could be made of a Soviet artist, and one that would come back to haunt Shostakovich.

1. Beware of Music[1] (1929–1933): *Poor Columbus* to *The Counterplan*

Poor Columbus [Der arme Kolumbus]

Shostakovich's generally accepted first cinema score is *New Babylon*, but on 14 March 1929, four days before it opened, the Leningrad premiere of Erwin Dressel's opera *Der arme Kolumbus* had included two extra pieces by Shostakovich, one of them for an interpolated animated film that was an anti-American plea for international peace. Even though he had been given little time he came up with *The Entry of the Yankees*,[2] part of which was good enough to recycle in the weird revue *Declared Dead* [Uslovno ubityi, 1931][3] and the First Piano Concerto (1933). His contributions' spiky wit is typical of his 'wrong-note' incidental music at the time, with squeaking woodwind, farting brass and appropriately Sousa-like moments. It also features a telegraphic clicking, perhaps inspired by Erik Satie's *Parade* (1916). But his main concern was *New Babylon*, and he received a boost when Sovkino decided that the score merited universal performance.

New Babylon [Novyi Vavilon]

Soviet technology lagged behind the West and even by 1929 synchronised sound had not arrived, so cinemas still had live music, though frequent complaints about its quality led to a decision to 'publish scores by highly qualified musicians'.[4] But different musical forces – from solo pianists to full orchestras – presented difficulties, and Shostakovich may have planned a piano version for the musically less well equipped cinemas. Though critically praised avant-garde films were unpopular, Sovkino commissioned an avant-garde score, to be played by a large ensemble in synchronisation with a politically sensitive, avant-garde film. Obviously, everyone underestimated the political and practical difficulties that the film and its music would cause.

The directors had been working on *New Babylon* since February 1928,[5] and it was to open on 18 March 1929, but Shostakovich signed the contract only on 28 December, leaving less than eleven weeks to deliver the ninety-minute score.[6] Simultaneously he was writing music for Meyerhold's Moscow staging of Vladimir Mayakovsky's *The Bedbug* which Trauberg claimed was based on their idea for a film,[7] teaching in Leningrad and preparing a concert – and all this while suffering from flu. Commuting between the two cities, he wrote twenty-three items for the play and, after watching the film twice and timing each scene, delivered the piano score (Trauberg claims) after only two weeks. Shostakovich may have been helped by a familiarity with the idiom, though: according to Trauberg, he had seen FEKS's earlier films.[8] Unsurprisingly, the play and the film share some material, but he also drew on existing music by himself and others. However long it took to write, the 2,000-rouble fee was generous, about fifteen months of the average salary; together with his other work Shostakovich was well off.

Louise, a salesgirl at the emporium New Babylon during the Paris Commune, loves Jean, a French soldier. She joins the communards, but he capitulates and ends up digging her grave. The Commune was an important model for the Revolution, being pored over for lessons to be learnt, but the film provoked a storm. The Communist Youth International denounced it; the Russian Association of Proletarian Writers defended it; factory workers disagreed about it; and there were calls for public debates. Newspapers were divided, some urging their readers to see it and some even calling for the makers to be tried for 'jeering at the heroic pages of revolutionary history and the French proletariat'.[9]

The directors insisted that the music was integral to the film, but 'linked with the inner meaning rather than the external action and [developing] contrary to the events, independent of the construction of the scene'.[10] But the score's difficulties made orchestras keen to replace it with pot-pourris of old tunes, while conductors resented their lost arranging fees. Meanwhile, critics condemned its deliberately confusing sense of time and space, fearing it would alienate the masses, and the political controversy added to the film's problems. Sovkino's call for art to be 'intelligible to the millions' was rebutted by Trauberg as 'NEP-style ideology' and mere 'agreeableness in this battle with public taste'.[11] A week before the premiere Shostakovich wrote an article criticising the standard of film music and the conditions under which films were shown (illustration 1, page 8).[12]

1. *Sovetskii ekran*: Shostakovich's thoughts on cinema in 1929

It's time to take cinema music in hand, to eliminate the bungling and the inartistic and to thoroughly clean the Augean stable. The only way to do this is to write special music.[13]

Anticipating the controversy, he explained how he did *not* always illustrate the images:

> For example at the end of the second reel the important episode is the German cavalry's advance on Paris though the scene ends in an empty restaurant. Silence. But the music, in spite of the fact that the cavalry is no longer on screen, continues to remind the audience of the approaching threat (illustration 2, page 9). I constructed a lot of the music on the principle of contrast. For example when Jean comes across Louise at the barricades he is filled with despair. The music becomes more and more cheerful, finally resolving into a giddy, almost 'obscene' waltz reflecting the Versailles army's victory over the people of the commune. [...] While the rehearsal of the operetta is on screen the music plays variations of Hanon's exercises which take on different nuances in relation to the action; [...] Based on a wide variety of sources, the music maintains an unbroken symphonic tone throughout. Its basic function is to suit the tempo and rhythm of the picture and make the impressions it produces more lasting.[14]

2. *New Babylon*: the empty restaurant under threat from the Prussians

Shostakovich may have been aiming for a 'symphonic tone', but *New Babylon* is more akin to a wordless opera, the rapidly changing moods of its seven acts echoing one of his all-time favourite works, Alban Berg's *Wozzeck*, which he saw in 1927.[15]

One moment deserves particular attention: the extraordinary counterpoint of the 'Marseillaise' and the Can-can from Offenbach's *Orpheus in the Underworld*. More than once Trauberg claimed the idea,[16] but it is strikingly reminiscent of a passage in Dostoevsky's *The Devils*: 'The little piece, which, in fact, was rather entertaining, bore the comic title "Franco-Prussian War". It began with the menacing strains of the *Marseillaise*. [...] But suddenly mingling with the masterful variations on the national anthem [...] came the trivial strains of *Mein lieber Augustin*.' Dostoevsky anthropomorphises the themes until 'the horrible waltz' completely subdues the 'Marseillaise': '[I]t was Jules Favre sobbing on Bismarck's breast and giving away everything, everything. [...] [O]ne had a feeling of countless barrels of beer, the frenzy of self-glorification, demands for milliards, expensive cigars, champagne and hostages. [...] The Franco–Prussian War was at an end. Our young people applauded.'[17] The music's title, the counterpoint and the fact that Dostoevsky was one of Shostakovich's favourite writers leave little doubt that this passage was in the composer's mind, throwing up questions about how far he shared the novel's view of Revolutionaries. In the film their complacency and failure to build on early victories lead to their downfall, just as it had endangered the regime they were attacking. But the (in retrospect, unsurprising) Stalinist view was that the Commune's problem was a lack of centralised control. Reflecting that, a Party conference in March 1928 concluded that the Party should have an important role in the industry,[18] and earlier that year Stalin had taken the precaution of instigating the Shakhty trial, eliminating 'wreckers' who were sabotaging the economy, *pour encourager les autres*.

All this made *New Babylon* politically questionable, but the musical accompaniment was abominable. Part of the problem lay in the fact that Shostakovich had written his score for the film as it existed in December 1928; but, subsequently it was substantially re-edited. Whether this was 'less than three weeks' or 'three days' before the premiere,[19] he could not ensure that all the changes were transferred to the orchestral parts. He had foreseen possible difficulties in performance and at several points inserted optional repeats of a few bars or flexible moments such as drum rolls which could be expanded or contracted to allow the orchestra to get back into synchronisation with the film, but they could not compensate for the 24 per cent that was removed.[20]

According to *Testimony*:

> Films have meant nothing but trouble for me, beginning with the first one, *New Babylon*. I'm not talking about the so-called artistic side. That's another story, and a sad one, but my troubles on the political side began with *New Babylon*. [...] Things could have ended very badly and I was only in my early twenties then. And there was trouble with every other film.²¹

After the First Symphony and *The Nose*, the score for *New Babylon* was Shostakovich's third major leap forward, and as so often he uses quotation and allusion extensively, in this case including Revolutionary songs, Offenbach,²² Tchaikovsky and his own music.²³ Cinema accompanists (and perhaps Shostakovich himself) had long done the same thing; the 'Internationale' or the 'Marseillaise' would always get an audience joining in. But in *New Babylon* the quotations are more than time savers, quick scene painters or cues for knee-jerk reactions. Already he understood that, when images and music come together, they form a 'third genre'.²⁴ Though each is brilliant individually, the images and music combine to reflect on each other, making it one of the highpoints of Soviet cinema, of Shostakovich's career (and not just in film), and of dramatic music in general.

But a failed film's editorially messy music was not a candidate for publication. He did reuse part of it in his 1931 ballet *The Bolt*, though that suffered an even worse fate, lasting just one performance.²⁵ Other than that the music for *New Babylon* was put aside, and for many years the rare screenings were accompanied by piano improvisations: exactly what Shostakovich was attempting to overturn. Even so, it remained controversial, though Viktor Shklovsky wrote a cautiously supportive article in 1930.²⁶ In 1967 Piotr Sobolevsky, who had played Jean, criticised its unintelligibility,²⁷ and President Pompidou of France banned a 1971 broadcast on the centenary of the Commune as 'too revolutionary'. Conductor Gennadi Rozhdestvensky rediscovered the score in 1976, and in the 1980s the film's reputation was boosted by performances, attended by Trauberg, of a version prepared by the BFI and publishers Boosey and Hawkes. But there are still disagreements about it. The film was broadcast in Russia in 2000 with Shostakovich's music completely re-edited (anonymously), while Marek Pytel's video and book explain the rationale behind his synchronisation. Even the score is a matter of contention: the BFI performances used the version held, but not as yet published, by Boosey and Hawkes, which varies considerably from the Sikorski edition.²⁸

New Babylon was one of the earliest film scores to be written by a major composer, and it is certainly the most successful. Other composers began to be attracted to film when synchronised sound became possible, and the avant-garde, in particular, embraced it. This may be coincidental or it may imply that, though a flop, *New Babylon* was influential in showing some of the more far-seeing members of the industry what was possible. Among the composers who wrote for it in the next few years were Vladimir Deshevov (*A Fragment of Empire* [Oblomok imperii, 1929]), Vissarion Shebalin (*Men and Jobs* [Dela i liudi, 1932] and *Torn Shoes* [Rvanyi bashmaki, 1933]), Boris Liatoshinsky (*Ivan*, 1932), Gavril Popov (*K-Sh-E – Komsomol: Patron of Electrification* [K-Sh-E – Komsomol: shef elektrifikatsii, 1932] and *Chapaev* [1934]), Yuri Shaporin (*Deserter* [Dezertir, 1932] and *Three Songs of Lenin* [Tri pesni o Lenine, 1934]), Vladimir Shcherbachev (*The Storm* [Groza, 1934]) and Leonid Polovinkin (*Marionettes* [Marionetki, 1934]). Some of these (e.g. Popov) continued to work in the industry for many years, and members of the old guard also contributed – e.g. Reinhold Glière's score for the 1931 sound version of *The Earth Thirsts* [Zemlia zhazhdet, 1930]. But, at the same time, the increasing problems faced by avant-gardists meant that some of these scores are not particularly adventurous, and were, to some degree, taken on for the money. Nevertheless, the recent rediscovery of such composers has not, as yet, extended to this aspect of their work.

New Babylon crystallises many of the aims and effects of Shostakovich's music both in and out of the cinema throughout his career, but its failure meant that the makers had to prove that their hearts 'beat in unison with the millions'.[29] In 1930 Shostakovich signed contracts for Nikolai Akimov's staging of *Hamlet*, an operetta and Alexander Macheret's documentary *The Concrete Sets*. Accustomed to enormous workloads, he also embarked on his opera *Lady Macbeth of Mtsensk*, though he probably did not think it would take two years to complete. But he also declined a quasi-cinematic project, the Bolshoi's request for an opera based on Eisenstein's *The Battleship Potemkin* (Oles Chishko filled the breach in 1937).

Enthusiasm [Entuziasm]

Shostakovich's first encounter with sound cinema, if only from a distance, came in the minor flurry of films that followed Piotr Shorin's development of a sound-on-film system. Released in April 1931, Vertov's documentary *Enthusiasm* was mostly scored by Nikolai Timofeev, but, even though Shostakovich was not involved, it does use the last bars of his Third Symphony ('The First of May') – the first of many such borrowings.

Alone [Odna]

Before that, Kozintsev and Trauberg announced their next film *Alone* as the story of a soon-to be-married teacher (Elena Kuzmina)[30] being transferred to the Altai on the Mongolian border, but meeting such resistance from the locals that she gives up hope and commits suicide. Though Socialist Realism, which was to become the standard Soviet artistic theory, was yet to be defined, art was already expected to be positive and 'accessible to the millions'. But Lenin's view of its political role meant that artists had to divine what was needed to discuss properly past, present and an as yet undefined future. It was very easy to be too pessimistic or ignore current concerns, to produce work that was a mere 'epigone' of the past, or to commit any of a range of other sins. Nevertheless, at least partly by choice, the avant-garde was beginning to change, and the end of *Alone* was rewritten, with the villagers helping to rescue Kuzmina while she comes to see the value of her work.[31]

The FEKS label had been dropped, but *Alone* was made by the same people and is essentially an Eccentric production. Planned as a sound film, doubts about technology meant that it was shot silent, but the success of *The Road to Life* [Putevka v zhizn', 1931] (despite execrable sound) encouraged the studio to add sound. Realising that some of *New Babylon*'s performance problems stemmed from the long and inflexible cues, Shostakovich completely changed

3. *Alone*: 'How Good Life Will Be!' – An ironic comment on life in the Altai

his way of film scoring, producing small pieces that could be easily cut, altered and shuffled around – a technique he used in several future film scores. *Alone*'s kaleidoscopic soundtrack – a clever mélange of music, sound effects and speech – makes it one of the most innovative early sound films. As Kuzmina does her morning exercises, a jolly song is slowly invaded by the street sounds of the waking city, but for the Altai scenes Shostakovich took little direct account of indigenous music, though a shaman does appear, with his strange wailing and drumming. Perhaps in an attempt to avoid synchronisation problems, it largely avoids synchronised speech, but, despite some claims, there are intelligible voices, which the makers considered an 'important element'.[32] They often appear off-screen, but this can give them a God-like quality: cutting between Leningrad street tannoys and the Altai fills the entire country with news of Kuzmina's rescue, and after she receives her posting she returns to a shop she visited with her fiancé where a siren chorus of crockery urges her to stay.

The music also differentiates between Kuzmina and the Altai's village chief, the bey. He gets a musical gesture: trombone *glissandi* signifying his sloppiness and rejection of Soviet thought. Shostakovich reused the effect in various places, most notoriously in the detumescence of the sex scene in *Lady Macbeth of Mtsensk*, its meaning changing between contexts. Her developing personality is traced by the bouncy song 'How Good Life Will Be!' Trauberg claimed that the tune was his and that Shostakovich merely transcribed it. 'I wrote the song and instructed Shostakovich how to compose it, and he wrote it right away, a very good song.'[33] First it describes Kuzmina's *current* ecstasy at the prospect of her *future* wedding. Next it accompanies her watching the sleeping bey and his helpless wife, and realising that their political ignorance parallels her Leningrad past (illustration 3, page 13). Finally, as she is rescued, the line appears on title cards alerting us to her new joy in working for a *future* where life will be beautiful. Even in 1931 the song was at odds with reality for many, yet, though it seems to rub the audience's noses in their privations, the incredibly catchy tune seems to have been popular, as its lyric – simple repetitions of the title – gave a glimpse of the claimed end of their suffering. But the film was criticised for pessimism and portraying the shaman too sympathetically. Nevertheless, Stalin, on seeing it, decided to invest in sound for the film industry.[34] Later Shostakovich was dismissive, probably to distance himself from its 'formalism',[35] but had the clampdown on the arts not happened shortly afterwards *Alone* could have shown one way forward.

In late 1931 Shostakovich condemned Soviet music, citing 'abominable specimens' of clichéd incidental music, the low regard in which theatre music was held and poor sound quality in the film industry. Such work was 'a depersonalisation of the composer'. After 'reluctantly' finishing Akimov's

Hamlet he would forswear theatre work for the next five years, withdraw from the operetta and Macheret's film and dedicate himself to a major work: *From Karl Marx to Our Own Days*.[36] Given his love of Shakespeare, rather than terminate the contract he probably completed *Hamlet* far from reluctantly while, masked by the (never-to-be-written) Marx project continuing work on *Lady Macbeth of Mtsensk*.[37]

As he noted later, film-makers were working on how to combine sound and images,[38] and one question was that of form. If, in the wake of *The Nose*, *New Babylon* is a wordless opera, *Alone*'s kaleidoscope of many short pieces is more balletic, though its sound world often veers close to *Lady Macbeth* and the anguished Fourth Symphony that he was to write four years later.

The Golden Mountains [Zlatye gory]

One form in which Shostakovich had worked but which was not reflected in his film work was the symphony, but in 1931 Yutkevich's *The Golden Mountains* filled the gap. Inspired by and dedicated to the Putilov Factory strikers, the film is set in 1914 and shows the politically ignorant peasant Piotr coming to the city to work in the barely disguised Krutilov Factory, and being tempted to strike-break. Shostakovich knew that film scores should not be 'mere illustration', and, looking back, felt fortunate that directors such as Yutkevich and Fridrikh Ermler agreed,[39] but despite the move towards a more symphonic score he turned to song as he had for *Alone*. Not only did he come up with the catchy 'If Only I Had Mountains of Gold',[40] he based another on the popular song 'There Used to be Merry Days',[41] hoping to add to the film's success, though the novelty of sound would have attracted audiences in any case. Some of *The Golden Mountains*' music is close to pure sound, but the musical cues are more developed than in *Alone*. This made the suite easier to compile, but, oddly, he did not include the song. This proved so popular that, on the front page of a press book, accordion-playing actor Boris Tenin serenaded a young woman on a street corner, with the opening of the song (complete with Cyrillic text) written across the bottom of the page (illustration 4, page 16). 'It became all the rage,' reported Herbert Marshall.[42] The young Shostakovich had a penchant for slightly outré instruments (though he did grow out of it), and various early scores include parts for banjo, theremin and flexatone, among others. The bourgeoisie of *The Golden Mountains* are given an insinuating waltz, with the bizarre addition of a Hawaiian guitar. The boss's son plays it on the piano before setting off with a waistcoat – and a watch that plays the theme – to bribe Piotr to break the strike, and it accompanies a party celebrating a huge war order, but, even though it satirises the decaying bourgeoisie, its sheer infectiousness made it enormously popular. As well as

4. *The Golden Mountains*: the press book, featuring Shostakovich's music (courtesy of BFI Special Collections)

these popular pieces there was a more 'serious' one, a baroque fugue for organ and orchestra for a sequence that cuts between strikes in Baku and Petrograd though the scene was removed from the film's later re-release. This was a particularly unfortunate excision as, according to Arnshtam, 'the Fugue, with its iron step, suddenly lent such importance to what might have been thought a passing episode as to make it one of the film's central moments'.[43] I. Baudo, who played the organ on the soundtrack, agreed: 'apart from purely instrumental effects... Shostakovich has achieved much more – he actually wrote a brilliant piece in fugal style, in which the plastic theme was made an expression of a dramatic situation of the important episode in the movie.'[44] The soundtrack continues *Alone*'s innovations, and when a factory hooter blares out over shots of St Petersburg and Baku it urges the whole country to strike. As it still had to be shown in silent cinemas, there are also intertitles, but the makers turn this to their advantage for showings in sound cinemas. The music for 'The Boss Rewards His Workers' has a curious air of incomplete grandeur; starting with the 'fate' motif from Tchaikovsky's Fourth Symphony, we can hear that the great idea for breaking the strike is doomed to fail. The film had a rocky premiere as Leningrad's erratic electricity supply meant that the film ran too slowly and the music burbled along *basso profundo*, though this did not detract from its popularity. But the critics were not entirely convinced and the 'abstract' fugue was frowned on, as were the closed musical forms that related to the film's structure, yet this was exactly what was starting the new trend of symphonic film scores.

Qué viva México

Shostakovich may have had another close shave with cinema when Eisenstein returned home from Mexico in early 1932. American left-wing novelist Upton Sinclair had backed a film project, but they argued and he falsely promised to forward the unedited footage to Moscow. In 1957 Jay Leyda, an Eisenstein pupil then resident in the USA, showed it, with an introductory title card explaining that Shostakovich had been asked for a score based on Indian and Spanish music. But, according to another source, Leopold Stokowski met Eisenstein in Mexico in late January 1931 and agreed to arrange the music.[45] There have been several attempts to reconstruct the film, but none has used music by Shostakovich, and he never worked with Eisenstein.

The Counterplan [Vstrechnyi]

In January 1932 Yutkevich and Ermler were instructed to make a film in the new 'industrialisation' genre, which included Vertov's *Enthusiasm* and climaxed in 1932 with Macheret's *Men and Jobs*, Dovzhenko's *Ivan* and Esfir Shub's *K-Sh-E: Komsomol – Patron of Electrification*.⁴⁶ The tribulations of *New Babylon* seemed long forgotten and Shostakovich's cinema career was in the ascendant, but the film industry was in increasing trouble: output had been catastrophically reduced, from a record 128 films in 1930 to 74 in 1932, and the following year further Party criticism brought it down to just 29.⁴⁷ In April 1932, as the script was being written, the various creative groups were restructured into single unions, facilitating the further control of artists.

Vstrechnyi is usually translated as *The Counterplan*, referring to the contemporary slogan 'Let's have a counterplan to the industrial and financial plan', as factories responded to their set quotas with even greater proposals.⁴⁸ It was the only film commissioned to celebrate the fifteenth anniversary of the Revolution – and one so important that Leningrad Party chief Sergei Kirov took an interest in it. Yutkevich directed the younger cast members and the older Ermler looked after the more senior characters. As a former member of the Cheka (forerunner of the KGB), perhaps Ermler was also expected to look after other aspects of the production, but he later claimed to have had little interest in the subject.⁴⁹ The father of conductor Mark, he remained a friend until his death in 1967.

Much of *The Counterplan* is formulaic, with various 'types' of society obviously represented by the characters. The wrecker Skvortsov endangers the work of a Leningrad turbine factory, but his sabotage is discovered and corrected by good communists. Babchenko, though good-natured, is a little too fond of his vodka and works unscientifically and inaccurately. Vasia is an insightful Party leader and his friend Pavel an eager pupil – an early example of the Party, embodied in a leading character, teaching someone to become a better communist, a model that became common in Socialist Realist art. The directors tried to soften things by having Vasia and Katia as husband and wife, and some of their scenes are very natural, but his claim that 'if numbers are against the fulfilment of the plan, then they are hostile numbers! And the people who bring them forward are not our people but they are enemies!' is spoken so enthusiastically that one wonders whether it can be entirely serious.⁵⁰

According to Stalin, 'wrecking by the bourgeois intelligentsia [was] one of the most dangerous forms of opposition to developing socialism',⁵¹ and in March 1931 several alleged Mensheviks were arraigned for sabotage. It became a common theme in art, and in Shostakovich's ballet *The Bolt* a drunken wrecker is foiled by good workers. Both the ballet and the film support the 'unmasking of wreckers', though the makers had little choice: writing to a friend Shostakovich described the ballet as 'shit, but compared to [the proletarian composer] Davidenko, it's Beethoven'.⁵² But, whereas the ballet lasted only one night, the film was a hit – though not without a struggle.

It was criticised at an October screening at Sovkino, and re-edited for its premiere on 7 November 1932 (the fifteenth anniversary of the Revolution), though this did not save it from further criticism for unoriginality after its release.

As with his two previous films, Shostakovich wrote a song for *The Counterplan*, working hard on it to produce his biggest cinema hit to date – and, had he known it at the time, of his career. The lyrics are a simple call for workers to 'meet the cool of the morning' and go joyfully to work, but it was undoubtedly the tune – a brisk march – that caught people's imagination. Shostakovich had a knack of writing these infectious melodies, and none is more so than this one, with its simple rising and falling outline. Its popularity attracted envious accusations of plagiarism[53] but it became a model, though the similarity of Tikhon Khrennikov's 'Parting' in the film *At Six o'Clock PM After the War* [V shest' chasov vechera posle voiny, 1944] is undoubtedly unconscious. That popularity must initially have been an urban phenomenon as less than 1 per cent of projectors were equipped with sound, so rural audiences would not have heard it, though radio broadcasts may have helped

5. *The Counterplan*: all problems are resolved by returning to work

its popularity and the sheet music was published in 1933.[54] Just as he had varied Hanon's exercise in *New Babylon*, so for *The Counterplan* he wrote orchestral, choral and solo vocal versions of the song, including one in the style of a melancholy Russian romance and an upbeat folky one, both accompanied by guitar, interleaved with orchestral pieces, as in *The Golden Mountains*. As so often with his incidental music, he raided it for other works, in this case the unfinished operetta *The Big Lightning*, though for the minute he left the song alone. 'Finally the melody's author becomes anonymous, something of which he can be proud,'[55] Shostakovich later observed, laconically echoing the drive against individualism, and implicitly pointing to popular song's democratic nature. On a more practical note he added that '"The Song of the Counterplan" has taught me that music composed as an integral part of a film must not lose its artistic value, even outside it'.[56] But the song is less than the soundtrack as a whole, which is one of the most interesting to which he contributed.

The credits are accompanied by a brief fanfare followed by the song, roughly sung by a choir, into which the orchestra gradually intrudes, taking over for a driving and serious brass-led middle section, which gives way to a heavy tutti recapitulation of the song. Having heard it from the masses we then hear it from Pasha's fiancée Katia, as she gets ready for work.[57] But, despite *The Counterplan*'s political conventionality, its soundtrack continues the experimentation of *Alone* and *The Golden Mountains*, going further in smudging the line between music and sound effects, using factory noises as a percussive underlay to the etched and often dark music. It did not go unnoticed: despite Soviet technology's inferiority, a sympathetic American critic described the sound as 'excellent',[58] and a British one thought the final reel 'provides one of the finest instances of the dramatic use of sound that we have seen' (without mentioning Shostakovich or the music).[59] For another the 'noise-apparatus' and 'use of electrical instruments and special sound-effects interwoven with the music presents quite new sensations to the ear'. The Soviet Union was 'about to solve the problem of film music, both serious and light, in a form that will correspond in quality to its pictures'.[60] Babchenko's breakfast is accompanied by a mechanical humming, but back in the factory we hear 'proper' music again (the song), though when Babchenko is given a kitten the factory noises mingle with a grotesquely grunting tune in the brass, which slowly coalesces into a sentimental melody for a small group of winds. The proletarian 'The Song of the Counterplan' is contrasted with Alexander Dargomyzhsky's romance 'I am Sad', setting a text by Lermontov. Sung by Skvortsov's mother while he comments on the rise of Marxism, the lover's lament ('I am sad because you are happy') is turned into a weird political critique. The love story proper is a troubled one: Pasha secretly loves Katia, who explains her dissatisfaction with Vasia as they walk through Leningrad's White Nights (now and then in misty-eyed soft focus). The long complex cue starts with an over-sweet version of the song, which segues into a perky 'morning' scherzo and then into a broader, flowing romantic melody, with cyclists going to work and a bizarre ballet of steamrollers. Katia talks about how to save her relationship with Vasia. Pasha hides his disappointment, but his emotions can hardly be reflected by the song's easy return, completing a confusing journey with the implication that concentrating on work will solve the problem (illustration 5, page 19). At the end of the film a mass rendition of the song celebrates the factory's successful fulfilment of the plan, while Skvortsov, having at first clapped along 'enthusiastically', cowers in a corner.

Weighing the subject matter against the film's success, Shostakovich must have had mixed feelings. These would have intensified after a 1933 film conference, when *The Counterplan* was held up as a model for Soviet film-making, and further confused when lyricist Boris Kornilov was purged in 1938, and his wife, the poet Olga Bergholtz, beaten by the NKVD until she miscarried. Nevertheless, the song was an important element in his career for many years (though it was later described as a setting of a folk text) and he reused it, seemingly as a reminder to the regime of his ability to write popular, politically acceptable works.[61] It also kick-started the phenomenon of the song score, which would become an almost constant strand in Soviet film music.

2. Intelligible to the Millions (1934–1939): *Ankara – Heart of Turkey* to *The Great Citizen*

The repressions reflected by *The Counterplan* intensified, exploding on 1 December 1934, when Leningrad Party chief Kirov was assassinated. Stalin launched an investigation, and, fuelled by more or less enthusiastic support from many people, the numbers of those implicated and arrested spiralled surreally into the thousands. Ironically it seems that Stalin knew perfectly well who was behind the killing, having ordered it himself to remove an increasingly popular rival and rein in Leningrad's independence. Kirov's involvement in *The Counterplan* must have given Shostakovich pause for thought: would he be deemed one of the 'conspirators'?

Ankara – Heart of Turkey [Ankara – serdtse Turtsii]

But, cinematically, he was an asset, being approached to write more scores,[1] while more of his concert music was appropriated for films. Esfir Shub and Yutkevich's *Ankara – Heart of Turkey* [1934] combines documentary footage with acted scenes while the soundtrack mixes Shostakovich with traditional music; in one scene a semicircle of people embroider clothes while 'sazandari' musicians play Middle Eastern instruments and others dance a rhythmic warlike dance.[2]

By 1934 Shostakovich was getting into his cinematic stride but he was not alone, that year is one of the highpoints of Soviet film music. Prokofiev was at the centre of three of the best; in his own *Lieutenant Kizhe* [Poruchik Kizhe] the synchronisation between music and images suggests a close collaboration with director Alexander Faintsimmer though he disagreed with his suggestion of a grotesque score, producing instead a light parody of classical style. The soundtrack was conducted by Isaak Dunaevsky who was developing his own cinema career, and wrote the score for Alexandrov's immensely popular musical *Happy Guys* [Veselye rebiata] and they would dominate the genre for several years. It starred Leonid Utesov with whom Shostakovich would produce *Declared Dead*. Dmitri Kabalevsky's score for *A St Petersburg Night* [Petersburgskaia noch] is largely developed from a single melody, a technique that appealed to his mentor Prokofiev but was rarely used by Shostakovich. Beyond that, Shaporin scored Vertov's *Three Songs of Lenin*, attempting (with admittedly varied success) a mixture of his own music and pre-existing pieces.

The Tale of the Priest and His Worker Balda [Skazka o pope i ego rabotnike Balde]

Having worked with four directors, Shostakovich added a fifth with his first full-length cartoon, Mikhail Tsekhanovsky's Pushkin adaptation *The Tale of the Priest and His Worker Balda*.[3] A priest employs a simpleton for a year in return for being punched three times. But he worries about the payment, so his wife suggests setting an impossible task to escape it. Balda is sent to collect an imaginary debt from the sea devils, but manages to get the money and returns, knocking the priest over and advising him not to be so cheap. Apart from Pushkin's popularity (especially in the run-up to the 1937 centenary of his death), the story of a simpleton outwitting a priest probably appealed to the keenly atheistic state,[4] but the film had many targets – for instance a drunkard sells pornographic postcards parodying the gently erotic paintings of Kustodiev, such as *Russian Venus*. Given Shostakovich's friendship with the artist (who had died in 1927), his work on this 'completely anti-Kustodiev' project[5] is a mark of his nihilistic state of mind. Around the same time he wrote his First Piano Concerto, which, with parodies of Beethoven and Haydn and a dreamily waltzing slow movement, has a finale that stamps the classical coda into the ground with ruthless satire.

As with many animated films, the images were fitted to the soundtrack, giving Shostakovich a greater degree of control than usual. But work progressed slowly; he wrote it piecemeal over twenty months, mainly in late 1934, and reorchestrated parts of it in 1935 – a rare instance of his returning to a work, perhaps inspired by the prospect of a concert performance of a suite. The long gestation reflects the slow progress of the animation but its satirical approach was also a problem. In stark black and white, with characters' movements interlocking mechanically, it was seen as unPushkinian: it lost the 'high principles, the manner and style of Pushkin's story',[6] and the studio stopped the production. Despite this, Shostakovich, for some reason, continued to write music on the subject, perhaps hoping to make something else of it.

Most of the film was destroyed in the bombing of Leningrad in 1941 and only a few minutes survive.[7]

Around this time Shostakovich's satire was at its most extreme, lashing out in many directions and drawing on popular music, and this is one of his most enjoyable scores. The marching overture features bombastic timpani with a nasal trombone slithering over a twisted tune, while 'The Procession of the Obscurantists' is a tiptoe march for winds and xylophone. Late in life this was one of several early scores that Shostakovich considered revisiting, though nothing came of it.[8]

Obviously, it was unwise to be associated with projects that were criticised, but in the case of *The Tale of the Priest* the problems mainly rebounded onto Tsekhanovsky, who was demoted until 1939, when he was allowed to make *The Tale of the Silly Little Mouse* [Skazka o glupom myshonke], again with Shostakovich.[9] Expecting criticism for *The Priest*'s levity, Shostakovich covered himself by enthusing about the film, describing the music's farcical, fairground atmosphere and explaining that humour in music was just as valid as lyricism, melancholy and tragedy.[10] Though *Alone* had been criticised, *The Priest*'s

6. *Love and Hate*: despair at the treatment meted out by the Whites

problems were the most serious his film career had faced since *New Babylon*, and this must have been particularly disappointing given his enthusiasm for the project and after the popular success of *The Counterplan*.

Love and Hate [Liubov' i nenavist']

At the same time he was working on Albert Gendelshtein's *Love and Hate*, a dark and intense drama that did little for his reputation. In spring 1919 General Denikin's White forces overrun the Donbass, forcing the women to work in the mines, but, faced with a Red counter-attack, the Whites retreat and decide to blow them up. However, the women's guerrilla action stops them, saving the mines for the Bolsheviks. Even allowing that the plot largely excludes men, Gendelshtein's sympathies are obviously with the women, who are sensitively drawn, particularly in the controversial sub-plot about one who has an affair with a soldier.

Like many Soviet films of the time, it stands on the crux of silence and sound; there are long stretches without any dialogue whatsoever, and much of the story is told through the interaction of the images and music. The women's morale-boosting song is Shostakovich's first extensive use of choral music in film, but other numbers show his real colours. A loutish soldier preens himself, so oblivious of his own ridiculousness that he even sings along to the comically bumbling march that plays on the gramophone, and the machine reappears in a darker scene that also relies on the music. To a record of a particularly ingratiating waltz, the soldier sympathises with a woman: 'Our lives are hard' – a crude seduction that succeeds only in reducing her to tears, which he sees as capitulation. Excitedly removing his socks, he accidentally throws one onto the gramophone, stopping the music. We then see the aftermath, stormy, trill-filled music reflecting her despair as she weeps on her bed (illustration 6, page 24), abruptly stopped by the return of the march cranked up to cruder and more exuberant levels. More cartoonish preening shows that she is now his domestic and sexual servant, and his climactic claim that he wants 'a good life' (reminiscent of *Alone*) tops one of the most satirical scenes Shostakovich ever contributed to.

But much of *Love and Hate*'s score has a darkness and implacable determination that is most reminiscent of a much later piece, the Eleventh Symphony (1957). It is only in the funeral procession for the martyred leader that the music's level of inspiration sinks, but the following preparation for battle, with its isolated crescendi – pillars between which are strung screamed dialogue and horses' hooves – reintroduces a weird and threatening atmosphere. Sound cinema 'expands the frame' by including the sounds of events that happen off-screen, and *Love and Hate* uses this new technique, as well as one that was familiar from *New Babylon*. An earlier attack is shown only by its effect – bullets raking a lake – but this is not just a technical innovation; it sets up the idea of an invisible enemy. The final scenes intensify this as Shostakovich's grim music struggles for glory but is ultimately ambiguous, while we see a long, static shot of the sky, using *New Babylon*'s 'principle of contrast' – the threat is present but unseen. A gunshot is heard. Only now do we see the 'enemy', which turns out to be the returning Red Army, heralded by a weird noise that sounds like an orchestral decrescendo played backwards. This is repeated at the start of the brief last sequence, which looks up from the ground as horses gallop overhead while a male choir's march is peremptorily cut short by the end of the film and the same cymbal crash that closed the credits, leaving a dangerous conclusion: however enthusiastically the Red Army is welcomed, the women coped very well on their own.

Though astonishingly photographed and edited, and with an innovative score that embraces broad satire and subtle illustration, the best that can be is that *Love and Hate*'s March 1935 release did not attract much criticism. However, that was no reflection on its quality but simply that it was overshadowed by the first masterpieces of Socialist Realist cinema: the Vasiliev Brothers' *Chapayev* [Chapaev] and, initiating a trilogy, Kozintsev and Trauberg's *The Youth of Maxim*. Like some of Shostakovich's scores, for *Chapayev* Popov combines symphonic sections with popular songs, adding a White Officer playing Beethoven's Moonlight Sonata (with an orchestral underlay).

The Youth of Maxim [Iunost' Maksima]

Shostakovich was Kozintsev and Trauberg's regular composer, and, just as they moved away from Eccentrism, so his style became less grotesque. The *Maxim* trilogy follows a Soviet 'everyman', who begins his political education in prison in 1910, returns as a Bolshevik agent in 1914, and in 1918 heads the National Bank. A working title was *The Till Eulenspiegel of the Vyborg Side*, after the popular but politically charged character. The Vyborg side was the northern, working-class district of St Petersburg. Shostakovich and the directors spent a month discussing the music and listening to accordionists to find Maxim's 'theme tune', eventually choosing the heartily swinging waltz 'Whirling and Twirling', though the text concentrates on amorous rather than political adventures. Despite this involvement, Shostakovich's credit for the first instalment is only for 'Music for the Prologue'. The song is used insistently and became so closely associated with Maxim that when Boris Chirkov was persuaded to reprise the role in the first part of *The Great Citizen* [Velikii grazhdanin, 1937] he sang it to reveal his true identity beneath the 'disguising' moustache.[11]

Intelligible to the Millions (1934–1939)

The Youth of Maxim opens with the hero singing his song while walking into focus. Impressionistic photography is a FEKSism that the trilogy retains, but more important is its ironic outlook. These features diminish as the trilogy progresses, but Shostakovich began his original work on it with a bang. The edge-of-the-seat night-time sleigh ride is paralleled by a brilliant combination of 'Oira Polka', the 'Krakowiak' and the favourite gypsy melody 'Dark Eyes', trumping *New Babylon*'s double counterpoint (illustration 8, below). Into this he slips 'I am a Footballer'!; a female goalkeeper exuberantly tells how she let in a goal, with a great thwack on the timpani. Given Shostakovich's lifelong addiction to the game, setting the text must have amused him.[12]

The trilogy relies on song to drive the narrative and help its popularity, as favourite folk and Revolutionary songs often occur at key points, in a way reminiscent of early cinema music. One of the most important uses of music is to mask Revolutionary activities, the first of several such uses in Shostakovich-scored films. Maxim signals the location of a secret riverside meeting by casually playing 'I Like Fishing on a Sunday Afternoon' on the guitar, though when he is captured he drops it, temporarily losing his 'voice'. Another meeting is masked by a party; the 'Oira Polka' is played on the accordion, an instrument that in countless films signifies the honest Russian, or brings consolation or encouragement. Kozintsev said they wanted to raise it to a tragic plane – that

7. *The Youth of Maxim*: the midnight sleigh ride

is to remove its 'low-art' associations[13] – yet, when Natasha's maths lesson (itself masking a lesson in Revolution) is broken up by the police, a student uses one to make a comically insolent noise.

Maxim's political journey begins when a fellow worker is killed in a factory accident and the funeral procession sings the Revolutionary song 'You Fell as a Victim', whose melody repeatedly leaps upwards only to fall back again. There is a stand-off between the militia and the workers. The eerie silence is broken when Maxim's drunken friend staggers into the street playing 'Whirling and Twirling' on an accordion, but the time for the happy-go-lucky proletarian is past and it is an ironically inappropriate song and instrument for this moment of intense seriousness before a pitched battle breaks out. Shostakovich's use of the iconic 'You Fell as a Victim' stretches a long way before and after this. In 1917 he, his mother and his Revolutionary aunt Nadezhda were among the many mourners who went to Petrograd's Field of Mars to bury 184 victims of the February Revolution. Along the way the crowd sang the song, and at home that night the eleven-year-old Dmitri played it on the piano. He would use it in *The Great Citizen* with a generic 'Revolutionary tragedy' meaning. But when he returned to it again in 1957 for his Eleventh Symphony he seems to have been genuinely fired by its passion, using it to condemn tyranny in the wake of the suppression of the Hungarian uprising.

The second of the film's two large 'choral' scenes is set in prison, and, when a fellow inmate is carried off, all the prisoners gradually join in singing 'Be Brave Brothers', another song he would reuse several times.[14] This visibly heartens the prisoners, including a girl whose performance can at best be described as approximate; the niceties of performance are as nothing beside her enthusiasm. But the guards move in and phrase by phrase the song is silenced. These two long cues are given to unaccompanied voices, a serious, self-reliant and particularly Russian medium. They sit at its centre, relentlessly driving home the ideas of self-sacrifice and defiance. But the soundtrack also includes some more experimental moments, on the border between music and noise, as when factory hooters surround the disconsolate hero – perhaps a reminder of the *Symphony of Sirens*, a Moscow-wide performance on ship and factory horns that had celebrated the sixth anniversary of the Revolution.[15] Shostakovich included a hooter in his Second Symphony (1927) and it was an effect to which he would return. But at the end of the film, when Maxim embarks on his Revolutionary life, we hear 'Whirling and Twirling' once again on the accordion. He has travelled from youthful apolitical enthusiasm, through political education, to a synthesis of the two.

After being finished, *The Youth of Maxim* encountered problems, and at one point it seemed as if it would not be released. Apart from its inappropriate levity, its title (at that time *The Bolshevik*) may have been a problem: was it worthy of such a weighty title?[16] The directors wrote an article claiming that any success would be due to a variety of reasons, including 'the people whose lives we found so moving'.[17] When it finally appeared, it vied with *Chapayev* for popular and political acclaim, but in the end it was a score draw and both became heroes. Chapayev, driving his tank into battle with a Lenin-like outstretched arm, or explaining strategy with the aid of a few potatoes, appeared everywhere, while Maxim became so popular that people wrote asking his advice on their problems, and one Siberian town even voted for him to be their parliamentary representative![18] But the most important endorsement came from the Kremlin. Kozintsev recalls watching the film with a running commentary from Stalin. 'Yes. No. That's good... yes.' Kozintsev could not understand which elements of the film were pleasing or displeasing the dictator, until he realised: Stalin was not criticising the film, but commenting on it as if it were reality unfolding before him. Fortunately for all concerned, he approved.

The Youth of Maxim has a number of elements, both in the music and the action, that would recur in future films, and not just those scored by Shostakovich. As well as using music to mask political activity, Shostakovich sometimes later drew heavily on folk and Revolutionary songs, not just for colour or to court popularity but to make political points – ironically, just as he had done in *New Babylon*. Other common features include the condemnation of alcoholism and the appearances from political mentors (stand-ins for the Party), until, at the height of Stalinist cinema, the intermediaries were dispensed with and the advice came direct from 'the leader and teacher'. Though these were not features over which Shostakovich had control, they do indicate the political climate in which he worked.

Fighters [Bortsy]

The Shostakoviches had always had an open marriage, but in early 1935 Dmitri began an affair with an interpreter, Elena Konstantinovskaia – a relationship that grew until the summer when, under the strain, he and Nina divorced. But by the autumn they were back together again; Nina was pregnant with their first child, Galina, and *Lady Macbeth* was continuing its massive popularity. In late 1935 he was offered the film *Fighters*, but even though it had not started in earnest this unlucky production was already onto its second director (Gustav von Wangenheim, after Joris Ivens), and Shostakovich was the second composer after Hanns Eisler. But the production dragged on and events in Shostakovich's life intervened, so that by 1938, when it was finally made, Hans Hauska was chosen as composer.

Meanwhile, Shostakovich had written a cello sonata and was performing it in Arkhangelsk when he read a *Pravda* review of *Lady Macbeth*.[19] Under the title 'Muddle Instead of Music' it described the opera as 'a deliberately discordant and confusing stream of sounds', 'a cacophony' and 'a deliberate attempt...to dissociate [classical opera from] simple and popular music, understood by everyone'. It was '"Leftist" chaos and '"Meyerholdism" infinitely multiplied', in which 'the power of good music to reach the masses has been surrendered to a petty-bourgeois "formalist" attempt to produce individuality by means of cheap buffoonery'. Given that the opera was a huge popular success both at home and abroad and had been hailed as a Socialist Realist masterpiece, this volte-face was as shocking as it was incomprehensible. It was followed a few days later by 'Balletic Falsity', a similar judgement on his ballet *The Limpid Stream*.[20] As unsigned editorials, these were more than the opinion of an individual critic, but the voice of the Party – there has been speculation that 'Muddle Instead of Music' was actually penned by Stalin himself. It was a shattering blow, and Shostakovich knew that his life was in danger: 'It is a game of ingenious trickery which may end badly'.[21] Like many others, he took to never leaving the house without soap and a toothbrush in case he was arrested, and for a while he slept on the landing so that his family would not be disturbed if he was picked up at night. Amidst the political problems there was the practical difficulty that his income was slashed by around 60 per cent. He was still earning ten times a teacher's salary but had a growing household and always financially helped less fortunate friends. The prospect of the other two-thirds of the *Maxim* trilogy must have been welcome, and other friends offered film work as well, making this his first intensive engagement with cinema. The eight films he had scored over the previous seven years were varied and he had brought an inventive approach to them, but some of the six films he would score over the next two years are musically more cautious and include some of his cinematic lowpoints.

Girlfriends [Podrugi]

One of the first musical events in Shostakovich's life following the denunciations was the opening of Lev Arnshtam's *Girlfriends* on 13 February 1936, though he had scored it before the storm broke. A fellow conservatory student, Arnshtam became Meyerhold's theatre pianist, recommending Shostakovich as his replacement when he moved into cinema, writing scripts and working in the sound department for *Alone* and other films. Developing a directing career, *Girlfriends*, the story of three girls who grow up together and go on to be First World War nurses, was his first solo effort.[22] The early parts of the score are played by a string quartet with the occasional addition of a piano and trumpet, texturally echoing the previous year's First Piano Concerto.[23]

Many cues are free of speech or effects, leaving the music as the emotional driver, and yet mostly it does not feel like a faux silent film. As the children of the village gather 'from every flat, from every corner', the sinuous string texture thickens, rising to a moment of harmonic tension for the confrontation with the moustache-twirling Tsarist officer, after which they run away to scurrying strings, perfectly amalgamating music, silence and speech. It does move closer to silent film in a long wordless scene showing the village's miserable poverty, a single repeated despondent note counting out the endless time (there is a similar effect in *The Golden Mountains*) before, with the mother's return, the music builds to an angry climax.

Again, a song plays an important part in the film. The girls go to the local bar, the Keys to Happiness, hoping to earn some money by busking. The name is doubly ironic; it criticises alcoholism, but the bar is ultimately the key to the girls' happiness as it is there that they start their Revolutionary paths.[24] A pianist pecks at the keyboard in Shostakovich's 'wrong note' style, supported by slithering strings. But the men are not interested in the girls' performance and throw them out. A Revolutionary takes them under his wing, becomes a political mentor and takes them to an isolated lake, where, aboard a boat, he teaches them the pre-Revolutionary song 'Tormented by the Lack of Freedom'.[25] A silvery nocturne, supported by pizzicato chords, is taken over and darkened by the piano for the move back into the bar, where, armed with their new repertoire, the girls win the men over and they join in. The militia arrive, and the men face them down with a defiant repetition of the song. As in *The Youth of Maxim* this song-scene is a long one filled with tableau-like compositions, showing that even young girls can contribute to the Revolution, and that the proletariat, acting in concert, can defy their oppressors. The years 1914 to 1919 fly by with the aid of twisty trumpet fanfares, later joined by a more conventional organ for a processional that leads them to adulthood and enlistment. This gives an opportunity for some war music, but the tension is increased as drum rolls blur into explosions, leaving the audience unsure if music is about to start or not. When it does, organ and timpani lugubriously combine and there is a shadow of the *dies irae* from the harp. In the middle of this, one of the girls declares her love for a soldier in an extraordinarily tender scene, with evanescent strings and an occasional splash of colour from the piano evoking both her tentative excitement and the snowy landscape.

But the martial theme returns with more quirky fanfares, like those he would write for *King Lear* [1970], the last of which marks Asya's death, before the film ends with a noble lament for the strings, which are later joined by the rest of the orchestra. As well as looking forward to future scores, there is a glimpse of his youthful irreverence as a careering train is accompanied by the 'Internationale' played on what sounds like a cross between a theremin and an out-of-control short-wave radio. This cheeky reminder of the dangers that Russia, but more importantly socialism, faced during the war must have increased the composer's anxiety, but it passed relatively unnoticed in the storm surrounding the opera and the ballet. Unfortunately, Shostakovich did not return to the music to make a suite, probably explaining why this, one of his best early film scores, is almost completely unknown.[26] The only disappointment is the conventional 'adventure' cue that accompanies the clichéd rescue of the girls from a pair of White Russian soldiers. Nevertheless, an excellent suite for a small ensemble could easily be compiled from the music, and some of the individual cues, if published, could make popular encores.

Like many other citizens Shostakovich was now constantly watched by the NKVD, who filed one report claiming he was close to suicide. But not all was gloom; in May 1936 his daughter Galina was born, and the Soviets knew that, in the composer, they possessed a valuable commodity. Certainly he was respected by the Left overseas; following the *Lady Macbeth* affair, prominent socialists discussed his situation and 'The Song of the Counterplan' turns up in Jean Renoir's propaganda film *La vie est à nous* [1936], and a few years later Nancy Head adapted it as a British left-wing hymn. Shostakovich's value to the regime became apparent in a peculiar way. Stalin's insistence that the film industry should develop its own recording technology rather than use the West's meant that, embarrassingly, it had hardly improved in six years, and there were still many silent cinemas.[27] In 1936 they negotiated with the United States on two fronts to correct this. In return for a supply of films they would receive modern sound equipment for all their silent cinemas. More intriguingly, according to composer and gossip columnist George Antheil, they approached Boris Morros, Paramount's newly appointed Russian head of music (later revealed as a spy), for the loan of Shostakovich in return for American sound technicians – 'men sorely needed in present-day Russia to judge by the hideous quality of their sound recording'.[28] But, for whatever reason, the deal did not come off; perhaps they feared that Shostakovich would reveal too much about events at home, or that he simply would not return.

The Golden Mountains (re-released)

In August 1936 *The Golden Mountains* was re-released, a reminder of Shostakovich's popular and politically acceptable work, especially as – in being cut by a third – it had lost that dangerous formalist abstraction, the fugue. But, as many Soviet films (including classic silents) were banned, this may reflect less its popularity than the need for films, even if they were re-edited re-releases. Perhaps inspired by Vertov's *Enthusiasm* the last bars of the Third Symphony end the film, accompanying a montage of marching strikers filmed from various angles. This had been 'introduced into the Finale' of the suite Shostakovich drew from the score in 1931,[29] implying that the film may originally have had different end music and the new coda retro-fitted onto it. Whatever the situation, the shortened version of the film seems to be the only one now available.

The Great Terror reached its climax in 1936 and 1937: plays were taken off, films stopped in production and around two million people were arrested, exiled or shot. Fame was no guarantee of security. The 'conspiracy' to murder first Kirov and then Stalin involved surreal numbers of people, prominent among them Stalin's long-time colleagues Zinoviev, Kamenev, their accomplices and eventually their relatives. Among those arrested, exiled or shot were Shostakovich's mother-in-law, his brother-in-law, an uncle, his sister, old flames Elena Konstantinovskaia and writer Galina Serebriakova and numerous friends and colleagues. Most shockingly Meyerhold's execution showed that international fame was no protection. Isaac Babel would die in 1939 or 1940, proving the futility of what he had wryly called the 'genre of silence'.[30] But it was already clear that this was not an option for Shostakovich: in the spring of 1937 he was called for an interview with the NKVD, only escaping when his interviewer was himself arrested.[31] Shostakovich had to write something. And it had to be the right thing. Having been officially 'advised' to withdraw his Fourth Symphony, he set to work on its successor (though the numbering would flag the existence of the earlier work), and scored *The Return of Maxim* and *Volochaev Days*. The November 1937 premiere of the Fifth Symphony was the most important event in his life since the launch of the First Symphony, but though, like the earlier work, it was a huge success it was not the overnight rehabilitation that has been implied more recently. However, it did begin the process, and the film work supported it.

The Return of Maxim [Vozvrashchenie Maksima]

The second part of the *Maxim* trilogy, released on 23 May 1937, must have raised his hopes of a political bounty. Shostakovich was promoted to 'composer' and there are several original pieces alongside the popular songs, but the music is much less structured than in *The Youth of Maxim*. Where that film had started with the best moment, the prologue of *The Return* is a conventional affair: 'Whirling and Twirling' performed by the hero, two friends and the proletarian accordion. The accordion turns up later in a strike-impoverished village, playing a distant relative of Maxim's song, which is taken up by a group of children who will apparently follow his example. After a simple march played by the military band on the streets of St Petersburg, we are thrust into the Duma in 1914 for the first of the political debates that mark the later parts of the trilogy. Even more strongly than in *The Youth*, *The Return* shows the necessity for Revolutionaries to use their cunning and, having begun his ascent and become a wanted man, Maxim uses the alias Fyodor. Again, music is used as a mask: in a tavern Maxim sings 'Fascinating Eyes' to cover a meeting with a contact before intervening in an argument between wild-haired Revolutionaries, like something from Dostoevsky's *The Devils*. Another debate (again in a back room) is masked by a quiet dance sequence, which includes a perky waltz that becomes a scene setter for the tavern and is used later as an ironic counterpoint to a ferocious argument and at the start of Maxim's billiard game with St Petersburg champion and bourgeois counter-Revolutionary Platon Dymba.[32] Maxim feigns incompetence, and the film is suddenly filled with FEKSian energy as the game is accompanied by an impertinently hiccuping polka. To gain Dymba's trust they sing, talk and drink (Maxim staying sober, unlike the intemperate hustler) before he cements their new friendship with a rowdy recapitulation of 'Fascinating Eyes'. Apart from these songs, Shostakovich includes a cue that, though short, is one of his most dynamic, taking us through a series of emotions in a single sweep. At dusk Maxim says goodnight to his girlfriend Natasha, but the music, rather than romantically describing their feelings or picturing the luminescent sky, is dark, speaking of an unseen impending threat, before working up to a militaristic toccato as Dymba attacks Maxim leaving him unconscious. The music dies back into darkness and is cut off by a morning factory hooter.

These voices of the proletariat return in a moment of Eccentric impudent humour, drowning a counter-Revolutionary's speech before the crowd sing 'Be Brave Brothers'. This leads to the most sonically interesting moment in the film, alternating elements of silent cinema technique with clever use of sound and music. A fight between strikers and police is conventionally scored, though the grimly determined scherzo is one of the score's highpoints. The police retreat and the strikers build a barricade. The frame is expanded by having the police return, but invisible, with their approach marked by the sound of marching. This advanced soundtrack technique is then negated with a barricade scene with tableaux that are reminiscent of *New Babylon*, and which is even topped off with a rendition of the 'Marseillaise' after which the death of the old worker is accompanied by a funeral march that moves from the lugubrious to the defiant. The strikers are defeated and the red flag torn down. But Maxim has the last laugh, joining the army to distribute Bolshevik propaganda as the accordion plays 'Whirling and Twirling', encouraging his fellow troops to sing along and sign up.

More developments in film music were seen in 1938, most notably with Prokofiev's score for *Alexander Nevsky* [Aleksandr Nevskii], a breakthrough in audio-visual montage, while Alexandrov's and Dunaevsky's success with

Intelligible to the Millions (1934–1939)   35

musicals spawned imitators including Ivan Pyriev's *Tractor Drivers* [Traktoristy] with music by the Pokrass brothers.

Shostakovich was working on the symphony upon which his future hung but still had to accept film commissions, while making the best of them in public. Four hit Soviet screens in 1938. *Volochaev Days* opened on 20 January, to be followed on 13 February by the first part of *The Great Citizen* (part two followed the next year) while the first days of October and November respectively saw *Friends* [Druz'ia] and *The Man with a Gun* [Chelovek s ruzh'em]. Not all of them are great scores, but there are parallels with his concert music, and it was not quite the automatic writing it has sometimes been portrayed as.

Volochaev Days [Volochaevskie dni]

The Vasiliev brothers' *Chapayev* was such a huge hit that their follow-up *Volochaev Days* could not hope to emulate its long-term popular success, though it was well received and generated lots of press coverage. It is set in 1918, when, latching onto anti-Bolshevik agitation in Siberia, first Japan, then Britain and the United States attacked the area around Vladivostok.[33] The film continues the idea of Bolshevism under threat from without, underlining the importance of building a strong Soviet state and exuding the paranoid air of the time; in June 1937 many party officials from the Smolensk area were revealed as German and Japanese 'spies'. It opens with an American journalist interviewing a Japanese colonel, praising his 'excellent English', though both pronounce every syllable of 'colonel'. The colonel's claim to be an amateur botanist visiting Russia to gather interesting specimens is accepted without question: the Japanese are duplicitous and the Americans are dupes. Later he demands that the Soviets sign a document, but it is in Japanese with no translation and they cleverly refuse. But, despite this portrayal, the film has a strangely conciliatory ending.

In a newspaper article Shostakovich described his current projects, briefly mentioning the forthcoming symphony but concentrating on his film work.[34] For *Volochaev Days* he admitted that there would be relatively little music as he intended to have a song running through it. Doubtless he hoped to repeat the popularity of earlier film songs, but he was satisfied only with the eleventh draft. At a conference on film music he played down the past, claiming that, apart from 'The Song of the Counterplan', he had not had much success with the few songs he had written, and hoping that the film's music would be more than illustrative, clarifying the events and the author's attitude to them.[35] At the same time he accepted the Kirov's commission for an operatic version, promising a large-scale heroic piece – adjectives that recur in his discussion of the song, the film and the opera. As there are manuscripts for over forty pieces of music – far more than appear in the film – he may have been planning to use the overspill in the opera, but in early 1940 he finally abandoned the whole idea. He also more or less seriously considered the films *The Great Citizen* and *The Young Guard* for this treatment.[36]

As Shostakovich promised, there is not much music in the film, but he clearly separated the two sides. The Japanese get oriental-sounding pentatonic music: a crude brass march, and little Japanese ditties that the colonel sings weakly and has difficulty finishing; the Soviets get more sturdy music, including 'The Partisans' Song'. But, rather than laying this contrast out in the credit sequence as a kind of overture, he actually produced an anonymous march, which is suddenly interrupted by the far more memorable song, making us wait for the Japanese music. There is one negative incidence of Russian music when three drunks sing in the street, one of them incongruously holding a bunch of flowers – a link to the colonel's 'interest'; alcohol is as big a threat now as the Japanese were in 1918.

In a grotesque scene the Japanese occupy a village and make a newsreel showing the 'friendly' villagers welcoming the soldiers with open arms and happily accepting their gifts, while the soundtrack is satirically filled with the brass's heavy pentatonic march. As soon as the newsreel is finished looks of disgust come over both sides, the 'gifts' are snatched back and the head of the village shot – a potentially dangerous comment on the reliability of film as a witness. As the gifts are returned the score finishes with a cheeky upward non-pentatonic flourish. The march reappears later when the Japanese torch a village, but this time the tail accompanies the grim visage of the colonel.

There are two battles, and the first starts, like so many of these set pieces, in a silent film style. Fanfares call each other across the snow, but the music moves out of the narrative into the score. The fanfares become less martial, more jolly, reminiscent of the music of *Alone*, and are filled with a lightly galloping dactylic rhythm (two short and one long note). One of Shostakovich's fingerprints, this became the basis of the finale of the next year's Sixth Symphony, for which this scene almost seems a sketch, and appeared in the Fifteenth Symphony (1971) by quoting the *William Tell* Overture. Finally, the Japanese are repelled from a hilltop with a giant snowball, and roll down accompanied by comically tumbling brass – a strangely anti-climactic end to the threat.[37] The hope may initially have been to deflate the Japanese threat with comedy, but it could still not be underestimated, and so the second battle is more serious and the music, including 'The Partisans' Song', more conventionally heroic, before the final rout (with the aid of a single tank) takes the level of musical inspiration down a notch. In a rare instance of a specific comment on his music Shostakovich said that it would describe the 'peculiar character traits' of Bublik the sailor and describe the psychological state of the characters when the White Guard meet the Japanese.[38] Unfortunately, he did not go on to explain this, but he may have had in mind the different music in the two battles.

Having portrayed the Japanese as heartless luxuriators, their departure is almost friendly. The leaders exchange gifts (a lighter and a cigarette case), the train leaves and they salute each other to the strains of Aturov and Parfenov's song 'Thro' the Dales and O'er the Hills'.[39] Shostakovich cheekily drew on this in 1947 for the cantata *Poem of the Motherland*, which, though published under his name, contained only one piece by him, *The Song of the Counterplan*. Though the promised opera did not materialise Shostakovich did get more value out of the film. When it was being prepared for a 1968 re-release he saw it again and was impressed enough with the song to use it for the middle section of his symphonic poem *October*, despite its celebrating an entirely different struggle. 'Quite unexpectedly I "heard" the whole of my future symphonic poem and set about writing it.'[40]

As well as four films scored by Shostakovich, 1938 saw conductor Yevgeny Mravinsky continue to promote the composer, recording the Fifth Symphony and being filmed conducting at least part of it.[41] Nevertheless Shostakovich hedged his bets by announcing a 'Lenin Symphony' though nothing came of it. Whether or not this was a serious proposal, it was a period of false starts as he also considered an opera based on Ilf and Petrov's *Twelve Chairs* and, in a bout of Lermontov-mania, operatic versions of *A Hero of Our Times* and *Masquerade*, and a ballet-biography of the poet.

Friends [Druz'ia]

Arnshtam's next production was *Friends*, which centred on the relationship between the Ossetians and the Ingush in 1916 – a potentially tricky subject, since Stalin was Ossetian, though he came from a different part of the region. Starting from a land dispute, it shows how long-feuding groups are brought together in friendly cooperation under the beneficent USSR, the implicit message being that national identity should be subsumed into the union. Even now, four years after Kirov's assassination, the film-makers thought it a good move to dedicate the film to his 'bright memory', and the character of Andrei was inspired by the leader.

Shostakovich did not write lengthy scores for some of the films from around this time, though this was not necessarily avoidance; many composers did the same. But *Friends* is a hybrid work; the first half often looks like a silent film, with many explanatory intertitles, though the ratio of dialogue to titles later changes. This gave Shostakovich room to write one of his most substantial scores, and one that should have driven the narrative forward rather than merely illustrating events. But it is one of his most disappointing: much of the music could have been by any of a number of composers, often merely anonymously accompanying the film – the very approach he had explicitly criticised. Not only is the film confused in terms of whether it should have a silent or a sound film aesthetic, but Arnshtam seems unsure of the tone in other ways. The opening is semi-comic – especially Nikolai Cherkasov's ridiculous overacting – and some of Shostakovich's cartoon-like music echoes this, but if he wanted to be 'funny' the broad comedy of the images left him little room to add anything. And when the serious (Russian) Andrei arrives the mood changes again.

Just as the film is a stylistic mixture, so the score is a similar ragbag of Shostakovich's current and older styles, alongside the local folk music, which was recorded in the Caucasus. He wrote that he was going to use folk music in the film, 'which I have not done before and it is interesting. I am closely studying the music and songs, mostly of the Chechens, Ingushes and Kabardinian-Balkars, and will base my music on them. Music will play a much more important role here than in *Girlfriends*.'[42] Despite this 'study' none of his own music is particularly redolent of the region, and this statement was probably a sop in the same way that his friend Ivan Sollertinsky had promised to study Georgian when he was criticised in 1936. Moreover, though he dismissed the music in *Girlfriends*, the score he wrote for *Friends* is in no way comparable to it. It contains some of the most anonymous pieces he wrote, though there are also parts that, while never rising to any particular height, are better. Perhaps the most interesting parts of the soundtrack are the local sounds and songs, which are completely separate from Shostakovich's music, and with which he was not involved. There are a couple of moments where he raises his game, and, strangely, one of these is the public meeting. These scenes usually brought out the least inspired side of Shostakovich, but he introduces this one with a series of implacable chords that predict its failure, and when later the two sides burst in they are heralded with brilliant chords in the manner of Janáček's Sinfonietta, though the music loses momentum towards the end, and after many speeches there is the inevitable 'Internationale'. Overall, *Friends* is an unhappy production, unsure of what it should be doing, and that is reflected in the score. Certainly it does not compare with *Alone* – another silent/sound film – or with *Girlfriends*, which has one of his most dynamic scores of the 1930s.

The Great Citizen (part one) [Velikii grazhdanin, seriia 1]

Nevertheless, *Friends* was not unduly criticised, which could be counted another success (though the later denunciation of Betal Kalmykov, on whose story the film was based, caused some unease), and Shostakovich went on to join Ermler's next production, *The Great Citizen*. The most morally problematic film Shostakovich worked on, it is, in essence, a justification for the purges. Telling of the assassination of a well-loved 'fictional' party chief (Piotr Shakhov), it transparently refers to the death of Kirov four years earlier. Ermler had difficulty getting it off the ground; it was seen as a handbook for assassination and actors were unwilling to portray the counter-Revolutionaries for fear of reprisals. But the real problem was that several senior people at Lenfilm, including Adrian Piotrovsky, the head of the scenario department, felt that the script was a falsification.[43] If they suspected Stalin of initiating the murder (as some did at the time) they could hardly expect the film to reflect that accurately, but perhaps they hoped to delay it until the whole thing was dropped. In the end, the situation was resolved when the entire Party organisation of the studio was arrested and several were shot.[44] This cleared the way for the film to go ahead, portraying the murder as the work of the opposition and arguing for complete obedience to the Party. The response to the film was positively ecstatic, and great swathes of the journal *Iskusstvo kino* were devoted to it. The timing could hardly have been better, since it acted to some degree as protection for those involved, including Shostakovich. In retrospect this approval was unsurprising, since the film was above reproach: Stalin, as he often did, had actually made extensive comments on the screenplay before shooting began. While praising its literary quality and its political literacy he drew attention to the 'errors', which included making the opposition too old (and presumably thereby a lesser threat) and comparing the nineteenth-century Revolutionary Zheliabov with the 'pigmy terrorists of the Zinovievist and Trotskyite camps'. The most interesting changes were that references to Stalin were to be replaced with the 'Central Committee of the Party' and that 'Shakhov's murder should not be the centre and highpoint of the scenario'.[45] Quite what the film-makers thought of these changes is hard to imagine: Stalin had increasingly featured in films but they were now being ordered to exclude him, and make the script 'correspond to reality' by downplaying the assassination of Kirov/Shakhov, removing the film's *raison d'être*.

Shostakovich can hardly have enjoyed working on *The Great Citizen*, however necessary it was, and as the purges continued to tear through the country he probably thought back to Kirov's interest in *The Counterplan*. Fortunately Ermler's striving for 'reality' meant that the film uses little music apart from what occurs within the narrative. The credits are accompanied by an all-purpose 'Revolutionary' march, swirling strings topped off with brass fanfares, but then at the end he introduces a more memorable idea and one he felt worth reviving in *The Unforgettable Year 1919* [Nezabyvaemyi 1919-i god, 1952]. But, as so often, we are immediately thrust into speeches and meetings discussing what is to be done, saving Shostakovich's pen. Later there is a party scene, which, as in the *Maxim* trilogy, covers a political meeting, and he wrote a little suite of dances, one of which came in useful later for *Cheremushki*; here it is enthusiastically thrashed out among a group of sentimental melodies, including 'Dark Eyes' played on the balalaika. Meanwhile, the discussion is about people in the Party who are stopping the progress of the Revolution – yet more wreckers who must be made to reveal their real motives in public. Whatever Ermler's political feelings – and he worked hard to get a controversial and potentially dangerous film into production – he did want to make an effective film.[46] With the various explanations (sometimes mendacious) of the events of 1925 it is a very wordy script, and he risks compounding the boredom by insisting on long takes. However, he makes it more cinematic by moving the camera, and there are some impressive visual moments, such as the public meeting in a crowded cinema. The counter-Revolutionaries try to disrupt it by pulling a fuse, but, exhilaratingly, it continues by the light of the projector. Sadly, Ermler seemed less concerned with the musical side, and this original moment is undermined by resorting to a cliché (the 'Internationale'), after which we cross town for more planning meetings and speech making, while outside a pot-pourri of marches is played by a street band. In the final scene Shakhov is hailed by a crowd, and the absence of Stalin, probably the result of his injunction, leaves the film with a strange feeling that something is missing.

In 1938 Shostakovich wrote very little outside the cinema, and, compared to its running time, *The Great Citizen* has a small amount of music. His claim that he wanted to write an operatic version can hardly be taken seriously and must have been put out as a smokescreen. Not only would the subject matter have disgusted him but the scant amount of music in the film meant that he would not be able to save himself work by drawing heavily upon it. However, Shostakovich was seeing his way slowly out of the woods, and his personal life took a turn for the better in May 1938 when his son Maxim was born.[47] By mid-1938 it was important not to let the momentum of rehabilitation slip, but he only started his next major work, the Sixth Symphony, in the summer of 1939. He seems not to have been in the mood to compose anything major, and with the political situation as it was that is hardly surprising.

The Man with a Gun [Chelovek s ruzh'em]

As the fifteenth anniversary of Lenin's death approached, a new genre emerged: *kinoleniniana* – films sanctifying Lenin. The encultment was being confirmed. But at his side was his right-hand man and natural successor, Stalin, beginning another cult. As the centenary of Lenin's birth approached in 1970 these films were re-released but without Stalin. Snipped scenes, new footage, optical effects and revoiced actors make him disappear, leaving Lenin as the original and unsullied political genius. Only now are they being restored to their original states.[48]

Yutkevich was a particular contributor to the genre, starting with *The Man with a Gun*, which began life as Nikolai Pogodin's script *November*, about a common soldier's life-changing meeting with Lenin. When pre-production ground to a halt Pogodin rewrote it as a stage play under its new title, and Boris Shchukin prepared to play the leader in both it and Mikhail Romm's film *Lenin in October* [Lenin v Oktiabre, 1937] (then known as *Revolt*), with both due to premiere in November 1937. Meanwhile, after *Pravda* asked why so many film scripts were being shelved and turned into plays,[49] the film was given the go-ahead to open in November 1938. But in April the madly overworked Boris Shchukin was replaced by Maxim Shtraukh. Shchukin died in 1939.

The play is built cinematically from many short scenes,[50] but the film has several longueurs, including a completely static scene of Shadrin and Lenin having a political debate in a corridor. Yutkevich rewrote this peculiarly uncinematic scene, turning it into stultifying inactivity, but contemporary reports see it as central, presumably because Lenin expounds his views at great length. Certain elements were becoming near-mandatory, including 'envoys to Lenin', in this case, Shadrin himself and a soldier's letter asking him to stop the war and solve the land problem, which also shows his understanding of ordinary people's concerns. Other common features include scenes of Lenin's omnipotence and humanity and, oddly, 'Lenin on the telephone' scenes.[51] The role of the first two is obvious; the last shows Lenin's contact with the whole population and is an extension of his omniscience and unruffled control. It also may refer to the technologisation that swept the Soviet Union after the Revolution and was therefore indirectly attributed to Lenin. But there are redeeming points: Shadrin's arrival in Petrograd is neatly signalled by a view of the Bronze Horseman (Falconet's famous statue of Peter the Great), seguing into a clock modelled on the statue standing on the mantel of the bourgeois house, while the chimes of a clock tower dissolve into the clock's smaller chimes. The penultimate scene, in which the soldier tells a friend his post-war plans, unaware that he is dead, is also touching, if unoriginal.

Again, Shostakovich wrote very little music for the film, but even this was uninspired. Like *Alone* and *The Golden Mountains* it has a theme song ('The Clouds Hang Heavy') though it appears only in the credit sequence, and he did not even compose the melody himself, leaving it to Pyotr Armand, one of the film's co-writers, scrupulously passing on the payment.[52] Despite this, in a 1955 radio interview he claimed to have studied Revolutionary songs to help him in the work.[53] There are just five pieces in the film, with the best being the second, 'October'. This covers Shadrin's journey to Petrograd, ending with eight chimes of the clock – incidentally, at half-speed: one stroke every two seconds. In its arch structure a lugubrious march clambers towards the light before falling back, the middle section accompanying Lenin writing *To the Citizens of Russia*, leaving the darker parts for Shadrin's journey. At the end of the film Lenin arrives at a factory to make a rousing speech, and after this we hear the finale, a perfunctory peroration, the first few bars of which are obliterated by a factory whistle. One other piece is worth mentioning. *Smolny* (cut from the same cloth as another piece with that name) does not appear in current prints and probably accompanied one of Stalin's now missing appearances, presumably the end of Shadrin and Lenin's conversation that originally also included 'the leader and teacher'.

Everyone involved in the film had done better work and some were under a political cloud, so it is hard to avoid the feeling that *The Man with a Gun* was an opportunity to prove their political credentials. It opened as planned on 1 November 1938 and was well received. Lenin's presence went some way to ensure this, and the cinema press carried positive articles with excerpts from the screenplay, before the complete script was published in 1949.[54] Yutkevich was awarded the Order of the Red Banner of Labour for it, and, though Shostakovich went unrewarded, he could chalk it up as a useful item on the CV. Like other films featuring Stalin *The Man with a Gun* was re-edited in the 1960s, but even in the midst of this political reorientation some things remained. Lenin still feels that the Bolsheviks were too liberal: 'We must shoot [our opponents] yet we put it off,' and that Trotsky is to be watched and one of his supporters arrested and tried.

The Vyborg Side [Vyborgskaia storona]

Released in February 1939, *The Vyborg Side* had been planned and scripted many months previously, and is a work steeped in the purges, though by late 1938, when Shostakovich wrote the music, they were beginning to slacken off as it was realised that the wholesale killing was damaging the country and Beria took charge of the NKVD, his predecessor Yezhov having disappeared. Like Eisenstein's *Alexander Nevsky* the major threat is Germany, but, whereas

Eisenstein drew parallels between the present and 1242, for Kozintsev and Trauberg the model was 1918. Both films hoped to rouse people against the Nazis, but *The Vyborg Side* risked reminding them of the capitulatory Treaty of Brest-Litovsk – tricky given that the secession of vast tracts of Russia to Germany was agreed by Lenin.

The Vyborg Side shows how the proletariat was not just involved in the Revolution but was its driving spirit under the guiding hand of Party symbol Maxim. It opens with him bursting through the doors of the Winter Palace, leading the Revolution – a scene that is echoed later in the film when he breaks in on a counter-Revolutionary meeting. The still-present 'wreckers' have now become anarchists and bankers, who, faced with nationalisation, frenziedly tear up the books, and obviously they must be dealt with ruthlessly. Kozintsev claimed that the pitched battles were based on events he saw in his youth in Kiev.[55]

Shostakovich was again 'promoted' and now shared a title card as co-creator with the directors (perhaps an attempt to help him with some reflected glory), but it is not a particularly extensive score, though there are some original pieces. Naturally, 'Whirling and Twirling' is there, and there needs to be music for the 'threat'. While this is ultimately from Germany, it immediately comes from an unsavoury alliance of the bourgeoisie and anarchists, which Shostakovich represents with a shabby brass band rendition of the 'Cannon Song' from *The Threepenny Opera*. One of its functions is to give them 'German-ness', but beyond that it may ironically reflect on the original, where Macheath and the Chief of Police reminisce about their time in the army ('soldiers live by their guns'). Just as they have perverted a noble calling, so anarchists have become enemies of the Revolution. Opposing Maxim's wholesome Russian melody, it becomes Dymba's theme, and he perversely sings it while playing Maxim's instrument, the guitar. Maxim's eternal enemy, he will do anything to hinder Bolshevism, wheedling, bribing, threatening and fomenting unrest. In contrast, Maxim, now head of the National Bank, discovers a surplus, and happily but calmly invites his colleagues to join him in 'Whirling and Twirling'. Oppositionists are prone to lose their heads at a moment's notice: calmness, or at most righteous anger coming from the knowledge that Communism would ultimately prevail is a sign of Sovietness. A baby is brought in, and it is decided to call him Vladimir after Lenin. Since christening was outlawed, the Soviet ceremony usurps Christian elements and, naturally, is accompanied by an accordion.[56] When Maxim arrives it breaks into 'Whirling and Twirling'; by now the whole city knows that this is his theme tune, and implicitly it will also be his surrogate son's. The soundtrack has several such simplicities, including effective moments such as the first scene in the Vyborg Side itself, where the hopelessness of the unemployed is underlined by complete silence, as a prelude to the factory hooters of the jobs that they want. One of the biggest pieces of music is the looting of the wine cellars (perhaps inspired by *October*) (illustration 8, below). Though it looks back at FEKS, with the looters comically covered with froth from broken champagne bottles, it lacks the wit in the editing. The music, too, combines a determined march with 'the Cannon Song'. Is the implication that, in destroying valuable champagne for no good reason, the Bolsheviks are in some way comparable to the anarchists? If so, the makers got away with what was too much in *New Babylon*.

But, overall, the trilogy was politically on the ball and immensely popular, and it was awarded a Stalin Prize in 1941. A Leningrad cinema was named after the hero and the public demanded more films, even about Maxim's as yet unborn children, but the directors had had enough and wanted to move on.[57] They were obviously favoured, as their next film was to be a biography of Marx – a subject untouched by Soviet cinema up to that point (though Eisenstein had considered adapting *Das Kapital*), and one the importance of which would have weighed heavy. Trauberg completed the script and Shostakovich would probably have written the score, but the project was aborted just as it was about to start. Shostakovich would have to wait until Roshal's *A Year is Like a Lifetime* [God kak zhizn', 1965] to tackle the subject.

8. *The Vyborg Side*: Maxim leads the assault on the wine cellars

Strangely, Shostakovich chose not to cash in on the popularity of the trilogy at the time, but waited until 1961 to ask Atovmian to compile a suite. What he delivered was a strange hodge-podge, excluding the best piece from the trilogy (the Prologue from *The Youth of Maxim*), the hero's song and everything from *The Vyborg Side*, but including a couple of pieces from *The Unforgettable Year 1919*, which was not directed by Kozintsev or Trauberg, deals with a different set of events and dates from 1951! If it was a sardonic comment on the interchangeability of elements in such pieces it falls flat, as the two interlopers stand out with their heavier, more pompous orchestration.

In 1965, like many 'classic' Lenin films, *The Vyborg Side* was 'restored' and Kozintsev took the opportunity to tighten some of the talk-filled scenes. But more importantly, he removed Stalin's appearances, taking care to leave Lenin alone, allowing it a new lease of life that otherwise it may have been denied. In one, the exhausted Maxim lies down to sleep, leaving a sign asking to be roused at 7. 'The most human of men' enters (originally with 'the leader and teacher') and they change the 7 to an 8, allowing him an extra hour's sleep.[58]

The Great Citizen (part two) [Velikii grazhdanin, seriia 2]

Also around 1939 Ermler planned *Second Symphony*, inviting Shostakovich to write the music. Little has been written on this unmade project, though there is a brief proposal on it dating from 1939 in Ermler's archive announcing that he hoped to make it in 1940 with his 'indissoluble little group, including the writers Bleiman and Bolshintov, the composer Shostakovich and the collective of actors and filmworkers with whom I always work'.[59] As it did not get very far he continued work on the second part of *The Great Citizen*, and Shostakovich provided the small amount of music needed. Part two of this epic is set in 1934, nine years on from part one – the year of Kirov's assassination and the seventeenth Party Congress, the 'Congress of Victors'. As in part one, Ermler attempts to tell some of the story cinematically and though there are still long static scenes of discussion there are some extremely free and lively camera movements, at one point panning around the 360 degrees of a construction site. Shostakovich claimed that music would be a major element in the film,[60] but in fact there is very little of it, just two major pieces. He must have known that with so much dialogue there would be little room for music, but, whether or not he expected to get off quite so lightly in terms of work, he was probably wrapping himself in the project as political protection.

The Sixth Symphony must have been on Shostakovich's mind around this time (the film premiered just six days after the symphony), and both its finale and the film's overture feature his much-liked dactylic rhythm. But, while the symphony's journey from dark to (apparent) light should have been just what was wanted, it was criticised for 'lacking a first movement', surprisingly, largely avoiding questions about the 'happiness' of the manic finale. No such questions surrounded the transparent overture to the film, though given the seriousness of the story this levity might seem surprising.

The other substantial item is, as Shostakovich explained, the funeral march, based on 'You Fell as a Victim'. Shakhov makes his way through the congress, happily greeting a stream of colleagues and well-wishers, before finally walking into another room and closing the door behind him. As in a Greek tragedy, the violent act takes place off-stage. With no preparation there is a sudden orchestral scream as a woman dashes out horrified by what she has witnessed. A momentary silence accompanies a card announcing the precise time of Shakhov's murder before the funeral march begins. The images hint at the funeral in *The Battleship Potemkin* but, unlike Eisenstein, Ermler concentrates on close-ups, stressing the impact of Shakhov's death on every member of society, eventually focusing on his mother. After this there is a eulogy, beginning – God-like – off-screen and culminating in a demand that enemies be shown no mercy, before a cursory piece of end music is played, which acts as a full stop but is not so substantial as to make us forget the importance of the preceding message.

The Great Citizen was a great event, rapturously received. The cinema press gave it huge coverage, and much of a contemporary book about Ermler was dedicated to the film (though Shostakovich went unmentioned).[61] But it was probably enough to be associated with such a prestigious and well-received film.

One commentator sees *The Great Citizen* as a loose reworking of Dostoevsky's *The Devils*, turning the Revolutionaries into counter-Revolutionaries, and, though film and novel do share some dialogue, it is not really clear why Ermler (who always attempted to follow the Party line), should have done this.[62] The novel had an ambiguous status at the time and an edition planned for the mid-1930s was suppressed, making it a dangerous choice and one that could not be publicised as a subtext. But this does not seem to be an Aesopian message: Ermler genuinely believed that Party guidance should be followed as far as possible (witness his description of *The Counterplan* as 'necessary' despite his having no feeling for it). This could be taken as a necessity for his career or for his political protection, but within the context of his work as a whole it must be seen as necessary for the furtherance of Party aims. Shostakovich did not share this attitude, either on *The Counterplan* or *The Great Citizen*, and the 'necessity' of the later film was to earn money and help confirm his rehabilitation. To have had so little to do would have been a bonus.

3. Interlude (1939–1942): *The Silly Little Mouse* to *The Adventures of Korzinkina*

The Story of the Silly Little Mouse [Skazka o glupom myshonke]

The late 1930s marked the first of Shostakovich's cinematic lowpoints, both in terms of quality and his enjoyment, but his next two films were happier experiences. In 1939 the now rehabilitated Tsekhanovsky made *The Story of the Silly Little Mouse*, with Shostakovich turning Samuil Marshak's verse story into a charming mini-opera. The baby mouse will not go to sleep. The mother's lullaby fails, and various animal neighbours – a duck, a pig, a toad, a horse and a pike – try to help with their own versions of it, but each is rebuffed with the refrain that their voices are ugly. The pig succeeds only in putting himself to sleep, and the catalogue of failure climaxes with the pike, who cannot make any sound at all. The cat, seeing a supper opportunity, feigns disinterest in order to encourage the requests for help. Where the others had attempted bribery ('Go to sleep and in the morning I will bring...') she simply asks the little mouse to go to sleep with soothing miaows, and the youngster succumbs to her 'lovely and sweet' voice. The cat moves in for the kill, but in a change to Marshak's original the dog intervenes and, after a victory march, everything is brought back to rights, with the mother recapitulating the lullaby and the dog's reminder that it is time to sleep.

The story is a natural for a musical setting, with the recurring lullaby as a chorus, alternating with episodes of recitative or pictorial scenes. Shostakovich paints the characters as vividly as Sergei Prokofiev had in *Peter and the Wolf* (1936), producing one of his most lovable scores. Tsekhanovsky produced far more Disney-esque images than he had for *The Priest*, and Shostakovich's music is correspondingly softer-grained. He uses the same style for *The Tale of the Fisherman and the Golden Fish* [Skazka o rybake i rybke, 1950]. The score by Yuri Levitin is in the style of Shostakovich's *Mouse*. But just as *Peter* – the hearty pioneer who proves his grandfather wrong and bests the wolf – is more than a story about a clever child, so there is a warning in *The Silly Little Mouse*: take care – even those who seem to have your interests at heart may have other agendas. With an awful, if unexpected, irony the Nazi-Soviet Pact was signed in August 1939, five months after Shostakovich wrote the score, and in June 1941, nine months after the film's release, the Nazis destroyed the peace with Operation Barbarossa.

In April 1939, a month after writing the score, Shostakovich wrote an article about it, explaining how he varied the lullaby for each character, though he does not make the obvious comparison with the Hanon variations in *New Babylon*.[1] Some other moments in the score are reminiscent of his pawky early style, particularly his theatre music. Perhaps he wrote the article expecting the film to be completed relatively quickly, but Tsekhanovsky was never one to hurry and concentrated on producing a beautifully animated film, full of humour.

With a firm script but no images Shostakovich could control the pacing of the story, and the extremely illustrative music comes together with the images more closely than in many of his other films. The film opens with a brief introduction, after which the dog announces bedtime and yawns before retiring; the warm, soft evening is captivatingly conveyed, and, throughout, such details are delicately sketched in both the images and the music. Though some twentieth-century composers produced unconventional-looking scores, Shostakovich was not one of them – the barless recitative from the Second String Quartet (1944) is a rare example, and even that was an experiment that others had tried long before.[2] But here some of the animals' parts veer a little way away from conventional notation: the duck's 'krya' is given headless notes, indicating the rhythm but not the pitch, while at one point the pig grunts (in fact 'khryoos') not quite a melody but a rhythm and a couple of different notes, and a few of his utterances are marked to be 'snorted'.

As the whole film is less than fifteen minutes long, Shostakovich concentrates on the lullaby. Working on *Lermontov* in 1942 Prokofiev argued that one theme should be repeated insistently, making it easier for the audience to remember and helping it become popular,[3] but Shostakovich had moved away from that approach since his early 'song score' films, marking an unexpected return. *The Silly Little Mouse* did not make an enormous splash at the time;[4] as a short children's film it would have been the support on cinema programmes, but Shostakovich retained a real affection for his collaborations with Tsekhanovsky, seeing them as 'film-operas' unconstrained by staging considerations – an idea to which he would intermittently return.[5]

Oddly, he used part of it again in 1960 in *Kreutzer Sonata*, the last of five Satires by Sasha Chorny, which opens by quoting his beloved Beethoven's sonata, soured to slight bewilderment. Later, the start of the mouse's lullaby accompanies the intellectual's first sight of the maid's calves, and the 'solemn moment' when they come together on the divan and 'You, the people and I, the intellectual, at last [...] will learn to know one another', perhaps again implying hidden motives, though who is the cat and who the mouse is unclear so perhaps he was simply recycling a good tune.

Concert Waltz [Kontsertval's]

The Silly Little Mouse was released in 1940, and in the same year Shostakovich played the waltz from *The Golden Mountains* in *Concert Waltz*, a surprisingly elaborate little film by Leonid Trauberg's brother Ilia.[6] As there is no piano in the original, Shostakovich takes the harp part, even though there are four of them in the huge orchestra, which Alexander Melik-Pashaev conducts.[7] This short segment must have taken some time to film as the orchestra is reseated for different shots, allowing the camera to follow the progress of the melody through various instruments, and the post-production phase was also complicated as there are sections where Shostakovich appears against vast back-projections of the players who accompany him, in the manner of Hollywood films such as *Fantasia* [1940]. Throughout the performance Shostakovich counterpoints the music's lightness and wit by glumly staring through his thick round spectacles, giving the impression that he would rather be anywhere else. After *The Golden Mountains*' 1936 re-release, to have another incarnation four years later is a testament to the popularity of the waltz. Indeed, it was 1953 before anything else from the score was recorded, and arrangements of the waltz continued to be published for many years.[8]

The *Kino-kontsert*, or 'film-concert', was a popular genre at the time, comprising cameos by famous Soviet performers, including ballet dancers, orchestras, singers and folk troupes, and some surprising items; *Concert Waltz* includes a jazz version of Strauss's *Tales from the Vienna Woods*. Shostakovich's music appears in several of them.[9] Apart from the entertainment value, the films showed the cultural strength of both high and popular art throughout the Soviet Union, and during the war reminded people what they were fighting to protect. But it was also a look back to Soviet *miuzik-kholl* whose heyday was in the 1920s and 30s.[10] The sections were also available separately, and *The Golden Mountains* section supported a 1941 London screening of *Valeri Chkalov* [Valerii Chkalov, 1941].[11] The mountain scene backdrop seems appropriate but was standard issue – David Oistrakh performed Debussy's 'La plus que lente' against a similar one in 1936 for another such film.[12]

The Adventures of Korzinkina [Prikliucheniia Korzinkinoi]

The late 1930s and early 1940s saw the rise of the epic Socialist Realist film, but Shostakovich turned away from such work, preferring to recapture his early vigour in Klement Mintz's short comedy *The Adventures of Korzinkina*, intended as the first of a series but the only one completed. The heroine is a harassed railway ticket clerk who takes pity on a hapless singer (played by the popular clown Musin), helping him to enter a talent contest. It is a kind of 'anti-*kino-kontsert*', mocking 'high art,' including Tchaikovsky's 'Dying Swan' (obviously already a staple target for anti-ballet comedy), and including a recitation of Lermontov that is interrupted by a series of increasingly bizarre comic events. The comedy is a mix of farce and slapstick, with more than a whiff of Chaplin, and Musin's scrubby moustache seems modelled on the comedian, who was so popular in the Soviet Union.[13] The stage manager is determined that Musin should not take part and chases him and Korzinkina around the theatre until the stage revolve is accidentally activated, causing chaos as characters are hurled from it. Musin eventually makes it in front of the audience, only to get stage fright, leaving him only able to whistle like Harpo Marx. But a kiss from Korzinkina enables an improbable bass voice to emerge from his slender frame, turning him into a winner with a performance of Mussorgsky's 'Song of the Flea' (orchestrated by Shostakovich), but which, as with *The Nose*, he refused to make musically 'funny'. After this he picks up his accordion to perform one of his own melodies, which is followed by Shostakovich's version for orchestra and chorus.

It was released on 11 November 1940, very soon after Shostakovich had completed the score. He probably wrote some of it before seeing the completed film; 'Restaurant Music', a piece for *New Babylon*-like chamber orchestra, incongruously accompanies the magician's act. But at times the music coincides closely with the action, suggesting that either it was played on-set to help shooting or the film was edited to the music. As with *Alone*, he made it as flexible as possible: the individual numbers could be cut up and shuffled as required, so that, brief as the published score is, there is more there than in the film.[14] But this meant rejecting a lot of very enjoyable music, and particularly mysterious is why the film-makers did not use more than a tiny fragment of the hilarious two-piano chase, which, with its sudden offbeat chords, fits the frenetic middle of the film as perfectly as the gently lachrymose final chorus does the sentimental ending.

In 1940 such light relief must have been welcome, and in early 1941 he also enjoyed composing music for Kozintsev's staging of *King Lear*, but in June the Nazis invaded and the Soviet Union embarked on the Great Patriotic War. 'The most important art' took on a new significance, being mobilised in various ways, and Shostakovich's film scores would be forced to change.

4. War and Cold War (1943–1953): *Zoya* to the Death of Stalin

Shostakovich's cinema style was usually in line with his concert works, but whereas some of his 1930s films had as little as ten minutes of music the later films often involved much more work, typically thirty to forty minutes. This might partly have reflected improving Soviet recording techniques and partly have been a fashion; other composers' scores were equally extensive. Large parts of Popov's 35-minute Second Symphony 'Motherland' were based on his score for *She Defends Her Motherland* [Ona zashchitaet rodinu, 1943]. Prokofiev's almost operatic *Ivan the Terrible* showed another way of constructing large-scale film scores. Some Hollywood composers were writing 'wall-to-wall' scores that ran virtually throughout the film, though this was something that Shostakovich generally avoided, along with 'underscoring' that quietly runs under dialogue. For some time he had largely, though not entirely, abandoned the 'song score' of *The Counterplan*, though they enjoyed a resurgence during the war as composers hoped to both serve the film and produce popular freestanding songs. Shostakovich was not always successful with either these or symphonic scores and not all of his middle-period film scores attain the highest levels of inspiration.

Zoya [Zoia]

Self-sacrifice for the state had been a prominent theme in Soviet art for many years (witness *Alone*) but in the war years it became much more urgent and much more heavily promoted, before, as in parts of the West, the post-war era was marked by a sentimentality for the years of hardship. *The Rainbow* [Raduga, 1943], *She Defends Her Motherland*, *Girl No. 217* [Chelovek no. 217, 1945] and *The Young Guard* are just some of the many films about people who suffer, and often die, defending the USSR. Many are young, continuing the idolisation of youth, and many are female, intensifying the outrage at Nazi atrocities and symbolising the violated *mother*land. Initially the sacrifices were implicit, as it was important to stir the population without disheartening them with too explicit deaths, but as the war progressed they subtly changed. By the time *Zoya* was released on 22 September 1944[1] a final push was all that was needed, so there was less risk of such propaganda being counter-productive; indeed, it became important in order to stress the inhumanity of Nazism. *Zoya* is not so much a biography as a sanctification of Zoya Kosmodemianskaya, a partisan who, at eighteen, was killed by the Nazis. With her fresh-faced optimism and plaits, the young Zoya could almost be modelled on Judy Garland in *The Wizard of Oz* [USA, 1939], but membership of the Komsomol and an androgynous bob transform her into a Soviet Joan of Arc. A perfect student, defender of her fellows, fearless in the face of the Nazis, she died a true martyr's death. The film was one of countless tributes; Matvei Manizer sculpted a 2.7-metre statue for Moscow's Izmailovsky Park metro station,[2] and literature included Margarita Aliger's Stalin Prize-winning epic poem and Pavel Lidov's *Tanya*.[3]

With an eye on populism, Shostakovich again began to reintroduce songs into his film scores, and 'The Song of Zoya' is a gently flowing triple-time tribute, with a hint of nobility without pomposity, despite the text ('A girl who has become a legend, who died and was born for eternal life'). His 1951 setting of approved poet Evgeni Dolmatovsky's poem 'The Motherland Hears' (with its, in retrospect, ambiguous opening: 'The Motherland hears, the Motherland knows') begins identically, and, courtesy of Yuri Gagarin, became the first song to be sung in space. Shostakovich was also careful to include a couple of famous tunes in the film. The opening sequence begins with the events leading up to Zoya's death at the hands of the Nazis, in a room strewn with old issues of *Pravda*. Zooming into a front-page report of Lenin's funeral, the photograph comes alive to the strains of a few bars of 'You Fell as a Victim', linking the fates of girl and Revolutionary. We cut to the (obviously Leninist!) baby Zoya and then follow her biography. Flashback structure was by now a formula, in the same way that 'historical' films began with the turning pages of a book. But to add 'authenticity' and keep us abreast of the chronology Arnshtam interleaves archive footage from historic events – the funeral of Lenin (1924), the completion of the Dnieper Dam (1932) and the welcoming parade of aviator-explorer Valeri Chkalov (1936). Zoya also has a dream/memory of a Red Square parade, watched by Gorky and Stalin (a brief shot survived the 1967 restoration), but the music is the innocently perky march featuring the flute rather than the brassy bombast that would actually have been heard.[4] While these interpolations are often well

War and Cold War (1943–1953)   53

integrated, when shots of Zoya and her friends are inserted the effect is more like Sergei Komarov's comedy *The Kiss of Mary Pickford* [Potselui Meri Pikford, 1927] or Woody Allen's *Zelig* [USA, 1983].

Essentially the story of Zoya's development into a partisan (her resistance work features only briefly at the end), the archive footage underlines the march of time, as do shots of loudly ticking clocks, dissolves and superimpositions. The schoolgirl Zoya, after a communist catechism, sits down with her diary: 'When I grow up…' she writes, and, dreamily chewing her pencil, she dissolves into her older self, while the music (which began with bold fanfares) drifts into a more romantic waltz, hinting at new concerns as she enters adolescence. But life is still a serious business, and the school's New Year celebrations are crudely cut short by footage of the Spanish Civil War, the Rachmaninovian piano music being explained when we see that it is actually a newsreel being accompanied by a classmate – a moment that must have amused the former cinema pianist. When Zoya reaches 'her seventeenth spring' we see her first romantic encounter: the young friends walking around Moscow while the music moves from tentative Tchaikovskianisms to more ardent music, underpinned by a throbbing bass before – as they enter Red Square – surging into the 'Glory' chorus from Glinka's *A Life for the Tsar* (Sovietised as *Ivan Susanin*),

9. *Zoya*: Zoya's pursuer vents his frustration

which has a theme of self-sacrifice that echoes that of the film. As so often, the pre-war years are portrayed as a time of vernal innocence ripped apart by the Nazi invasion, and we move inexorably towards Zoya's capture and a recapitulation of the film's opening. Zoya's face is superimposed over her partisan activities while the music is filled with rhythms and rasping brass reminiscent of the Eighth Symphony's wartime pictorialism,[5] looking forward to the scherzo of the Tenth Symphony.

However, the end of the film lacks any conviction. A montage of memories overlays Zoya's beaten face as she lies on a table. After a couple of clock ticks a heavenly choir breaks in and she sits up 'as the soul departs the body', resurrected, deliriously wide-eyed and inspired. Despite wearing only a thin shift and having her hands bound, she staggers into the snow pursued by a German soldier shaking his fists in frustrated rage, to the accompaniment of the thick brass fanfares and ecstatic choir that became the opening of the suite (illustration 9, page 53).[6] But she is recaptured and hanged, bravely pushing aside her captors to mount the scaffold unaided and urging her fellows to continue the fight. At the moment that the stool is kicked from under her Glinka bursts onto the soundtrack, and a barrage of newsreel footage shells the audience with images of victory, culminating in Zoya's radiant face superimposed over fireworks at the Kremlin. In these last few minutes the ridiculously overwrought plot, acting and music can, at best, be Arnshtam and Shostakovich going through the motions, undercutting the whole of the rest of the film, where they had tried to make Zoya a sympathetic character. Even though they had to show her as flawless, there are moments when one senses an inner life, perhaps stemming from Arnshtam's hope to show her 'lyrical' side.[7] The film was widely praised in the Soviet press, and Shostakovich's contribution was recognised – after a fashion; one critic praised the final 'life-affirming, solemn hymn', not realising that it was Glinka's,[8] while another simply described it as 'remarkable'.[9] One later paean of praise claimed that it overcame 'the dry, schematic concept of the scenario' and glorified 'the immortal deeds of the heroine', before whirling off in further hyperbole.[10]

But, while some of the cues are effective, and even though Shostakovich claimed to have 'adhered to the laws of symphonic development',[11] when Atovmian compiled the suite the many small cues proved problematic, especially in the introduction, stitched together from several pieces and with the seams all too clearly showing. As ever, though, Shostakovich was grateful. In late 1942 he had set six British poems, each with a different dedication; Atovmian, always a great support, received the first, a heartfelt setting of Raleigh's *To My Son*. One oddity is the suite's inclusion of the funereal Prelude, opus 34/14 in orchestral guise. Written immediately after *Lady Macbeth*, many of these twenty-four piano pieces use irony and different tones of voice to mask emotions, but this sombre, tolling piece is one of his profoundest utterances.[12] However, it does not appear in the film, maybe surplus to requirements, or maybe a victim of post-Stalin editing during the 1967 restoration; references to him in Zoya's interrogation scenes were not excised,[13] but a scene of him at Lenin's bier that is in the script was either not shot or cut later.[14]

Perhaps one reason that *Zoya* has few extended cues is Shostakovich's depression following the death, in February 1944, of his greatest friend and influence, Ivan Sollertinsky – a famous polymath who had introduced Shostakovich to much art and music. His death was an enormous blow, and Shostakovich decided to dedicate the Piano Trio he was writing to his memory. Composing it was difficult but, having completed it, he was soon worrying that he was composing his Second String Quartet too quickly.

Thousands Cheer

On the public stage the Seventh Symphony, dedicated to besieged Leningrad, had become a worldwide symbol of resistance, and fellow St Petersburger turned Hollywood composer Dmitri Tiomkin adapted themes from the symphony in the score he compiled for Frank Capra's *The Battle of Russia* [USA, 1943], part of the series *Why We Fight*. In New York, Stokowski and Toscanini tussled for the honour of presenting the Western premiere; Stokowski lost despite offering as an inducement a radio broadcast, a recording and the use of the music in a Hollywood film. As Shostakovich's music took on this role, he, by implication, joined it, appearing on the front cover of *Time* magazine, firewatching on the Leningrad Conservatory.[15] But with poor eyesight and of value to the regime he would never have been put at risk in this way. It was pure propaganda.[16]

Shostakovich's status as a symbol of resistance led in 1943 to film composer Bernard Herrmann being invited to play him in an unidentified film, though how serious the proposal was is unclear. In any case, Herrmann refused to be a 'cut-rate Shostakovich', and it was not made.[17] Meanwhile MGM's morale-boosting musical *Thousands Cheer* [USA, 1943] climaxed with 'The United Nations on the March' (actually 'The Song of the Counterplan') performed by a huge orchestra and a multinational choir, preceded by 'The Joint is Really Jumpin' Down at Carnegie Hall' in which Judy Garland mentions the composer ('They're playing/Tat-lee-a-ti, ta-tlee-a-ti/with Shostakovich,/ta-tlee-a-ti, ta-tlee-a-ti/Mozart and Bach').

Jose Iturbi, the film's musical director, wanted to include 'high' art, e.g. Kathryn Grayson singing 'Libiamo' from Verdi's *La traviata*. But the film still favours the popular, and when Iturbi begins 'The Joint is Really Jumpin'' with Lisztian flourishes Garland's bored distaste is softened as he slowly moves into boogie-woogie. Iturbi had begun his career as a concert pianist and he had played in Russia, so he may have met the composer, though it would have been before he wrote 'The Song of the Counterplan'. However it came to be included, the end of *Thousands Cheer*, ironically is reminiscent of Soviet 'concert films', with a procession of stars doing their turns. 'The Song of the Counterplan' was equally popular in the United States and the USSR; with Harold Rome's new words it was sung by a vast crowd in Madison Square Gardens welcoming Shostakovich and the Soviet delegation to the American Cultural and Scientific Conference for World Peace (25–27 March 1949), and New York City public schools' assemblies included it until the Cold War made it unacceptable.[18]

Once the war was over Shostakovich's popularity abroad had little effect at home, and the post-war years were among the darkest in his life as he was forced to accept film projects to keep him going financially, though they sometimes caused him immense trouble or deep frustration. This had begun during the war with a commission for Abram Room's *Invasion* [Nashestvie, 1945], based on Leonid Leonov's Stalin Prize-winning play of 1942, again concerning a character discovering himself in self-sacrifice; but Shostakovich dropped out, being replaced by Yuri Biriukov.[19]

Shostakovich's war work also included serving on the Art Council of the Committee for Cinema Affairs alongside twenty-four cinema workers, some of whom he had already worked with, and some of whom he would work with. Set up in late 1944, the committee also included composers Khrennikov and Shaporin, and two military advisers.[20] On 23 April 1945 the VOKS (the All-Union Society for Cultural Relations with Foreign Countries) Cinema Section set up a subsection for Film Composers and Film Musicians, and Shostakovich was also a member of that group. In the immediate post-war years one of its aims was to forge links with foreign composers, though in the atmosphere of the Cold War they concentrated on Eastern bloc ones.[21] He seems to have been relatively inactive, though he did write a few articles praising composers such as Béla Bartók and Witold Lutosławski.[22]

Simple People [Prostye liudi]

In the year of victory Shostakovich's Haydnesque Ninth Symphony was initially praised, before its 'lightness' was deemed inappropriate, he was admonished and it pointedly failed to win the Stalin Prize for which it had been nominated.[23] The film industry would not have to wait long to suffer even worse treatment. In 1944 Kozintsev and Trauberg had announced their next film, *The Storm* (not an adaptation of Ostrovsky's play).[24] It is a company piece set in an aircraft factory and culminating in an evacuation that is endangered by poor leadership. With Lenfilm closed for the war it was planned to make it in Uzbekistan, but shooting dragged on and it was the first post-war film finished back in Leningrad. It was reported as being in production in May 1945, and a release date of October was set.[25]

But *Simple People* (as *The Storm* was to be renamed) became embroiled in changing Soviet policies, and on 4 September 1946 the 'Decree on the Film *The Great Life*' was published.[26] Though only the second part of Lukov's *The Great Life* [Bol'shaia zhizn'] was explicitly banned, the second part of Eisenstein's *Ivan the Terrible* [Ivan Groznyi], Pudovkin's *Admiral Nakhimov* and *Simple People* were all cited and consequently withdrawn.[27] Neither Shostakovich nor the music was mentioned in the decree but it was trouble enough to be associated with such a production, yet three weeks later, on his fortieth birthday he was awarded the Order of Lenin. *Simple People* was finally released in 1956, so re-edited that the makers disowned it, but Shostakovich retained the opus number from the date of composition rather than release, even though none was published – nor has been yet. The delayed release of a wartime story may have caused the insertion of an introductory title card explaining that the events happened 'a very long time ago'.

In the little that has been written about the film various theories have been proposed for the ban. The depiction of child labour has been blamed,[28] but Trauberg said that it was simply 'not a good film'.[29] The lack of a real central heroic character with whom the audience could empathise may have been seen as another problem, but most striking is the number of downbeat, sentimental or hysterical scenes, and Moskvin's photography – dark, shadowy and rain-drenched – compounds the feeling of oppressive near-hopelessness. Even before its initially delayed release date of 1946 it was condemned:

> [T]he people are incapable of maintaining order and working in a sensible and organised manner. [...] The film fails to indicate the historical significance of the heroic labour of the Soviet people. [...] How many times has a hurricane been introduced into a film (even silent films) and how many times was the only purpose of this to make up for the film's lack of spirituality.[30]

Given that it was about inadequate working methods and that much of it takes place in harsh weather, climaxing with scenes showing how the factory copes with it, this was a sign that there was little hope for the film.

> The producers also try to show modern youth's love and write good dialogue; they use hackneyed literary allusion, making their heroine quote Juliet's monologue. [...] But even Shakespeare is powerless to help them. What was needed was something different – a profound, honest, truly artistic study of reality and a search for a form capable of giving an authentic reproduction of reality. This is the only real road to life.[31]

Shortly thereafter official anti-Semitism began to become overt, and Trauberg was accused of 'rootless cosmopolitanism' (i.e. being Jewish) and had to rely on pseudonymous writing. He later claimed that the regime wanted to attack a prominent Jewish director, and that, others having escaped, he became the 'leader of the cosmopolitans'.[32] It was the end of a directing partnership that had lasted since the early 1920s. Actors and technicians who had regularly worked with the directors had to choose between the two, and most, including Shostakovich, chose Kozintsev. Neither he nor the composer said much about the break. Trauberg claimed it was due to a mixture of anti-Semitism, Kozintsev's desire for a solo career and a disagreement over the film *The Actress* [Aktrisa]; Trauberg did not want the lead played by Sophie Magarill, the wife of Kozintsev, who refused to co-direct. But this was in 1943 and they continued to work together until after *Simple People*. Trauberg broke with Shostakovich in 1950, feeling that he had backed out of co-writing an operetta.[33] But letters show a misunderstanding; Shostakovich merely supported Trauberg's libretto to help get it accepted, intending to pass the composition on to Georgi Sviridov.[34]

The re-editing of *Simple People* makes it the most difficult of Shostakovich's films to discuss, as it is unclear how the new version compares with what the makers intended, but what exists is dialogue-heavy with little room for music, and there is no reason to assume it was moved around in the re-editing. What we are left with is a fascinating glimpse of what could have been, as far as the score is concerned, one of Shostakovich's darkest utterances on film.

The overture is a determined cue, with urgent rhythms in the brass and strings striving upward but followed by falling woodwind, and though there is another attempt at grandeur the cue peters out at the end, overtaken by the whistling wind of a storm – a sound that fills much of the early scenes and returns several times. Perhaps this premonition of nature's power put the authorities on their mettle about the rest of the film. While there are no direct quotes, it has some of the feeling of the Tenth Symphony, which was on Shostakovich's mind for some time before he actually wrote it. Pianist Tatiana Nikolaeva claims he was working on it in 1950 at the same time as writing the Preludes and Fugues, but while there are certainly similarities with several pieces from the late 1940s and early 1950s the case remains unproven.[35] The relationship between the Russians and the locals is inevitably a major part of the film, and early on two men meet. On the score we hear a woman's melancholy and unaccompanied ululation. Local music features elsewhere in the film, but as part of the narrative; this wailing reflects the despondency of the Russian but is expressed by the local woman. But the next piece of 'local colour' reclaims the republic for the Soviet Union, as a procession of locals is accompanied by a very nineteenth-century Russian view of the Orient, with exotic percussion and blaring brass; and this is compounded by the Russian, who, unable to see the strange, long horns, thinks they are trumpets. Asian exoticism was popular in the nineteenth century, and Shostakovich could draw on models such as Nikolai Rimsky-Korsakov's *Scheherezade* or César Cui's *Orientale* – the works that had proved so useful in his cinema pianist's exam in 1923.

The film's gloomy atmosphere becomes increasingly oppressive until it is relieved by a worker's dream sequence; work at the factory proceeds smoothly, and after a gently tolling harp a broad hymn-like melody breaks out against repeated violin notes before the brass climb upward in glory. The hymn hints at the opening of the Seventh Symphony, but, taken together, the elements and the melodic shapes echo the end of the Fifth Symphony – a work in which the 'glory' ending has now been discredited as a grotesque parody of rejoicing. While the tolling harp in the film does not reproduce the symphony, they share a common root in Shostakovich's Pushkin setting: 'A barbarian-artist with a drowsy brush/Daubs black over a genius painting/And his anarchic drawing/Senselessly scribbles over it.'[36] This is the very fate that befell *Simple People*, though we still await the moment when the 'foreign paints fall away like rotten scales'. Shostakovich may have been implying that the success of the factory was similarly illusory; an impression confirmed as the sequence does not end as might be expected, with another shot of the worker to bring us out of the dream, but goes straight into the next scene. Are we still in the dream? It is difficult to know whether this was the impression the makers wanted to give or a result of the re-editing, but in the next scene the exhausted boss sits in his office, sleeping and cradling the phone, to a recapitulation of the gently tolling opening of the dream music. The end of the film follows, with an adoring woman colleague discussing the glorious future and forthcoming generations to the rest of the 'dream' cue. We cut to a sleeping child as the rising brass theme blares out, and he opens his eyes. Perhaps the dream is over.

Pirogov

Around this time the biopic became a popular genre with Soviet film-makers. Given that the right unimpeachable (usually Russian) person was chosen, it seemed to be a way of speeding the process of script approval (though it could also work the other way). Usually simply named after their subjects, they include composers *Mussorgsky* [1950], *Rimsky-Korsakov* [1952] and *Glinka* [1946] (also honoured with *The Composer Glinka* [Kompozitor Glinka, 1952]),[37] the writer *Taras Shevchenko* [1951], *Admiral Ushakov* [1953] and scientists *Przewalski* [1951] and *Popov* [1949], who – it was claimed in Trauberg's original script – invented radio before Marconi, only to be cheated. The most notable is Alexei Meresiev, who lost his legs but continued as a pilot. Boris Polevoi's novel *The Story of a Real Man* [Povest' o nastoiashchem cheloveke, 1946] was adapted as a radio play in 1947 (a rarity at the time), and in 1948 Alexander Stolper's film and Prokofiev's opera appeared, the latter unheard until 1960.

Shostakovich worked on three biopics: the surgeon *Pirogov* [1947], the agronomist *Michurin* [1948] and the literary critic *Belinsky* [1950, released 1953]. The most important feature of these was that the hero often had no life outside his work, so Pirogov's entire existence is filled with his medical work, and Belinsky can think only of publishing liberal literary criticism. Dovzhenko recalled Stalin ordering that important people's lives should not be shown on screen: 'We ought to be interested only in the scientific [sic] and civic aspects of their lives.'[38] Even so, some of these films inspired more than mere hack work from Shostakovich.[39]

Pirogov, Kozintsev's first post-Trauberg film, is a biography of the surgeon who made his name in the Crimean War. Unsurprisingly, he was not only a great innovator in his field but politically liberal. In retrospect Kozintsev was unhappy with the whole thing, but it won a Stalin Prize in 1948, which must have been a relief after the failed Marx project and *Simple People*. At this early stage in the genre's history Kozintsev was attempting to do some interesting things with it, and there are some expressionist scenes and attempts at introducing satirically drawn characters, though they end up merely as one-dimensional caricatures, while Konstantin Skorobogatov speaks many of Pirogov's lines as if they were epigrammatic pearls to be savoured.

When it came to writing the score, Shostakovich took his cue from the military background, and a silvery, morning reveille occurs at various points. The other big element in the score is folk music, as, in the post-war years, *narodnost* (which can best – if clumsily – be translated as 'people-ness') became a touchstone of quality, making the 'People' the ultimate arbiters in many matters. Unsurprisingly, the film opens with a folk song, as Pirogov discovers a dead organ-grinder and his monkey, symbolising the threat to popular culture; later on, in a tavern, the exuberant band conveniently stops playing leaving a solo guitarist, every time there is a conversation. One of the best pieces in the score is a poised waltz, such as might be heard at a society event, though initially it underscores a series of cameos on a boating lake, where the constant conversations render it almost inaudible. However, it is later given its head by a band in the park, and it was seen as being potentially popular enough to record even before Atovmian made it the centrepiece of the suite. This is one of the few pieces of music to be part of the narrative; at other times the music is an odd add-on, the weirdest occasion being when a demonstration of an operation fails: an expressionist wind gets up (quite where from is never explained), with swirling strings and hammering side drum describing the desperate efforts to save the patient (illustration 10, below). Pirogov's visit to the town fair is equally strange, with grotesquely twisted fairground music as he sees a piece of frozen meat, which inspires another medical breakthrough. But the Sebastopol scenes return to visual and musical conventionality, with cautiously creeping strings marking the run-up to attack before the same theme blares in the brass for the short battle, the inconclusiveness of which is reflected in the music's hanging ending. The end of the film is similarly ambiguous, the silvery fanfare fattening to a thrashing climax and Pirogov looking forward, but with a shadow falling over his face.

As the post-war atmosphere darkened, Shostakovich turned again to his old hit 'the Song of the Counterplan', using it to celebrate the thirtieth anniversary of the Revolution as the final movement of the cantata *The Poem of the Motherland* (1947). No more than a collection of old pieces by Shostakovich and others, it properly moved people towards 'the firm determination to sacrifice oneself for the Motherland'.[40] It was rushed into print, broadcast on radio and recorded. But the Union of Soviet Composers' general secretary

10. *Pirogov*: a malevolent audience enjoys Pirogov's failed demonstration

Khrennikov judged it inadequate to the task and it was not performed live until 1956. If Shostakovich was hoping to stave off criticism by using his eternally popular song he had failed, but he would revisit it in 1948 with the film *Michurin*. In the meantime, the cantata's failure would be a shadow at the forthcoming Composer's Union meeting in early 1948. This marked Shostakovich's second great denunciation, as Culture Minister Andrei Zhdanov attacked the major figures in Soviet music, including Prokofiev, Nikolai Myaskovsky and Aram Khachaturian for writing formalistic, anti-people music.[41] Old scores were bought out for re-examination, and cinema music was not exempted, using the Decree on the Film *A Great Life* as evidence. The score of *Simple People* was one of a number of 'formalistic cinema-music tumours', which included Prokofiev's music for Alexander Faintsimmer's *Lieutenant Kizhe* and Popov's *A Severe Young Man* [Strogii iunosha, 1934] – an interesting comparator given that, since the film was still banned, few would have heard it.[42] Nikolai Bogoslovsky was criticised for modelling his work on Shostakovich, and, when it came to *Pirogov*, the editorial asked why it had not been noted that Shostakovich had repeated his old errors, 'compounding the unideological, stylistic tendencies in the work of Kozintsev'.[43] Most of the major composers had music banned, and even the acceptable pieces were rarely performed. A rare instance was at the Plenary Session of the Composers' Union in December 1948, when one of the few pieces by the condemned composers to be played was a selection from *The Young Guard*. Perhaps this was an indication of the kind of works that were expected; nevertheless, Khrennikov reminded him that, good as the score was, Shostakovich should not ignore other genres.

Yet other avenues were closed and when he was sacked from his teaching posts, as before he had to fall back on cinema work simply as a way of earning money. Speaking to conductor Kirill Kondrashin later he said that such work should be accepted only in times of extreme poverty.[44] At the end of the year he complained to Isaak Glikman that he found it completely exhausting: 'The ageing process is accelerating at an unheard of rate [...] after all, I did write a lot of film music last year. It got me something to live on, but it has entirely worn me out.'[45] Khachaturian was similarly affected and between 1948 and 1953 scored six films. Myaskovsky, almost uniquely, completely avoided such work. It must, then, have been galling when William Wellman used his music alongside that of Prokofiev, Myaskovsky and Khachaturian in *The Iron Curtain* [USA, 1948], the story of a Canadian spy network. As permission had not been sought, Moscow sued 20th Century Fox. Unsurprisingly, the US Supreme Court found in favour of the studio.

The Young Guard [Molodaia gvardiia]

But, before that, Shostakovich worked on Sergei Gerasimov's *The Young Guard*. Alexander Fadeyev based his 1945 novel on real events that had taken place in Krasnodon in 1942, when a group of young partisans fought the Nazis but were caught and executed. It won a Stalin Prize, but he was forced to revise it in 1947 and again in 1951, boosting the role of the Party.[46] Hence Party membership status is a touchstone, and the Party chief is regularly deferred to, immediately spotting the weakness of Stakhovich, who later breaks under torture and betrays the Young Guard. They, on the other hand, remain nobly silent and are killed by the furious Nazis. Gerasimov taught at the All-Union State Institute for Cinematography (VGIK, the state film school), and, though not intending to make a film, produced a sixty-scene stage version with his students. Many of them went on to appear in the film, taking it so seriously that they visited the area and spoke to friends and relatives of the murdered youths, before, on 29 June 1946, seven scenes were shown at VGIK. The film was completed in 1947, and Shostakovich sketched some ideas before finishing the score the following year. Meanwhile, Gerasimov had to re-edit it to make it acceptable, doing such a good job that it won a Stalin Prize in 1949, and many of the participants were also honoured. Even so, the panicked response to the German advance was criticised, though not as severely as that in *Simple People*.

Given the nature of the story it is unsurprising that much of the score is dark, but many of the cues progress from there to another mood, be it lighter and more determined (as in the credits) or, in the scene of the Nazi attack, exploding with rage. Contrasting with this essentially military music is a wan piece for strings, which accompanies scenes of loss. The subject does not allow much chance for humour but Shostakovich still manages to inject a touch. The Nazis (and the film is careful to differentiate them from Germans) are portrayed as irredeemably boorish, violent, thieving and with terrible table manners. Even worse, they sing an off-key version of 'Stenka Razin' and claim that the Volga is now a German river. Accompanying their entry into the town is a banal oompah march which, a few years later, much adapted, would serve as the starting point for 'A Drive Around Moscow' in *Cheremushki*. The most curious cue is when the Young Guard attack a POW camp and free the inmates. It starts with a guard being ambushed and killed, but rather than the predictable 'creeping' music transforming into something more exciting we hear quite jolly music, which becomes more intense only as the prisoners are freed, before a brief recapitulation and a grand finale that tapers away. Whereas, most of the time, the music is in step with the plot, here it looks forward to the freeing of the prisoners before the tension of the actual escape.

At the end of the first part of the film the partisans eagerly gather round the radio to hear Stalin praise their work, and this inspires them to an orgy of destruction, blowing up bridges and trains to the accompaniment of the driving brassy music that Atovmian would use in the suite's introduction.

On 25 October 1948, two weeks after part one had opened, audiences got a chance to see the second part of the story, though this is less satisfying, looking back to earlier films. The soundtrack is similarly retrogressive, reminiscent of the *Maxim* trilogy's extensive use of folk songs, even featuring a scene like that in *The Return of Maxim* in which messages are tapped out on a jail wall and the inmates sing a heartening song in the face of the guards' cruelty. Music is also used as a cover for resistance, with a cabaret detaining the Nazis while a building burns, becoming a desperate *Totentanz*, struggling to keep them from discovering the arson for as long as possible, with the Young Guard even going as far as performing a German song.

As before, there was a chance to get extra value from the score, and Shostakovich spoke of writing an opera on the same theme, but he later revealed that he had 'put everything into the film and nothing was left for the opera'. Since Yuli Meitusa had written an operatic version in 1947, this may have been a bluff. He also said he also hoped to write a symphonic work dedicated to the heroes, but that too remained unwritten.[47] Atovmian prepared a suite in 1954; but that was not quite the end of the music. There is a four-note 'march to death' motif, which, in part one, crops up briefly in a dark cue as Russian prisoners are forced to dig their own graves, and is more extended in part two. This became the basis for the start of the First Cello Concerto (1959) towards the end of which it is pointedly coupled to a quote from 'Suliko', Stalin's favourite song. It is also one of the network of quotes in the valedictory Eighth String Quartet (1960), though he did not mention it in a letter to Isaak Glikman.[48] The film winds up weakly, with a montage of newsreel footage of the Soviets overrunning the Nazis and a peremptory scherzo. Despite its references to Stalin the film stayed in favour, and in 1965 it was honoured with a six-kopek stamp.

Michurin

Shostakovich's next film was another biopic, but, despite its title, the spirit behind *Michurin* is not the agronomist but his pupil Trofim Lysenko, who denounced Mendelism and theories about genes and chromosomes as reactionary. His theory, based on Marx, Engels and Michurin, was that learnt behaviour was genetically transferable, meaning that once one generation of Socialists had been bred they would thereafter be self-perpetuating. The 'Michurin-Lysenko Path' had disposed of religious mysticism and superstition, and Lysenko began to dispose of his opponents. Michurin became the subject of yet another Soviet cult based on the self-created anti-Tsarist, pro-Party, proletarian myth which was exactly what the state wanted to hear.[49] His home town of Kozlov was renamed Michurinsk in his honour,[50] he was awarded Stalin Prizes and lauded by artists.[51] But behind the façade almost none of the strains he developed proved commercially viable.

Dovzhenko, feeling like an exile in Moscow awaited permission (which never came) to return to Kiev and hoped the *Michurin* would prove his loyalty. On a professional level, he could experiment with shooting in colour and time-lapse photography. He started adapting his play *Life in Bloom* in 1944 but it was repeatedly sent back and he wrote at least six different scripts. Fragments of some were published indicating that they went in and out of favour. One version was rejected for including too much of Michurin's personal life. The film was only completed in 1948. Stalin rejected it. Dovzhenko had a breakdown and went to a sanatorium to recover, after which he reworked it, with his wife Yulia Solntseva looking after much of the final part. Even then its release was held up until after the 1948 congress of the Soviet Academy of Agricultural Sciences, which celebrated 'the complete triumph of the Michurin Path over Morganism-Mendelism'[52] under 'the banner of Michurin's materialist biology',[53] now 'the sole correct line in the biological sciences'.[54] On the same day that the film was released (1 January 1949) Lysenko promised that his methods would bring limitless harvests and confound those who doubted the high quotas that had been set. In 1954 Dovzhenko wrote that 'evil forces surrounded me',[55] but Lysenko was causing deep divisions in the government as well. Despite being married to Stalin's daughter Svetlana, Yuri Zhdanov, son of Culture Minister Andrei, was forced to apologise for criticising Lysenko; and, when Dovzhenko got into trouble, Andrei – perhaps hoping to boost Michurin at Lysenko's expense – defended him.[56] Straight after Stalin's death Khrushchev severely criticised Lysenko, and in 1954 relieved him of his presidency, but somehow he stayed on as agricultural adviser until Khrushchev's fall in 1964.[57] It was at this time that Atovmian compiled a suite from the score of *Michurin*, perhaps as a pointed reminder of Lysenko's career, especially since Soviet crops had failed so disastrously in 1963 that wheat had to be bought from Canada.

Shostakovich was not the first-choice composer, but Popov's 'gloomy and hysterical'[58] score was criticised for its 'formalism and excessively complicated musical language',[59] so that 'even correctly reproduced Russian songs were distorted by the composer's harmonic refinements'.[60] In contrast Shostakovich's score made Khrennikov 'glad of its warmth and humanity'.[61] Dovzhenko is often portrayed as the great poet of Soviet cinema but he was also highly political though the crude lampoons are atypical and privately he disowned the film. Shostakovich was able to avoid these dialogue-heavy scenes and concentrate on pastoral scenes such as he did not usually get to score in films. *Michurin* has some marvellous photography, but sometimes the attempted grandeur of the music misses the pastoral element that a Dvořák or a Beethoven might have brought, and, generally speaking, the quieter cues are the ones that work better in the film.

Shostakovich also briefly resurrected 'The Song of the Counterplan'. Michurin's methods have been endorsed, and he sends a trainload of people to instigate them throughout the country (an early example of the 'virgin lands' policy, which would be the theme of *The First Echelon* [Pervii eshelon, 1956]). They leave singing the song, which will encourage them to over-fulfil the Plan, just as it did in the Leningrad turbine factory in 1932. Naturally, the song was included in Atovmian's 1964 suite, while Shostakovich, 'inspired' by a recent government resolution[62] and Stalin's reforestation scheme, included some of the film music in *The Song of the Forests*, which he regarded as a complete capitulation.[63] It won a Stalin Prize, leaving him richer but deeply depressed. Dovzhenko wrote more scripts including a science fiction story that he hoped Shostakovich would score, but he did not complete another film and died in 1956. Shostakovich expressed doubts about Dovzhenko's films in general but enjoyed working on *Michurin*, particularly admiring the photography,[64] but he would soon have to continue the series of war films with *Meeting on the Elbe*, *The Fall of Berlin* and *The Unforgettable Year 1919*. These are some of Shostakovich's least studied works, critics perhaps finding them an embarrassment politically as much as musically, yet the saturation level of propaganda – and how Shostakovich responds to it – is one of the very things that makes them interesting.

Meeting on the Elbe [Vstrecha na El'be]

Late 1948 saw another purge in Leningrad and open and official anti-Semitism, while the Cold War entered the freezer. The first two did not appear in films, but anti-Americanism was a constant theme. *Meeting on the Elbe* is set in Altenstadt, divided by the Elbe, and on the East-West German frontier during the last days of the Second World War, with the chaos being exploited by black-marketeers and the only honest brokers being the Soviets. Despite showing the friendship of a Soviet and an American general, it is a virulent portrayal of the United States as a continuing menace. In 1945 two lieutenants, the Soviet Alexander Silvashko, and the American William Robertson, were famously photographed together at the meeting of the two armies, but so quickly did international relations sour that by 1948 this was being downplayed.[65]

As director of such a film Alexandrov might seem a strange choice: he was Eisenstein's co-director and maker of a series of musical comedies starring his wife Liubov Orlova (*Meeting on the Elbe*'s American journalist-spy) with scores by pop master Isaak Dunaevsky. But they, of course, were equally politicised, though with a Hollywoodian charm that *Meeting on the Elbe*, with its crude visual caricaturing and tiresome music, completely lacks. According to Shostakovich:

> Writing the music was a grave task. I had musically to realise immensely important themes: the Soviet Union's victory, the tragedy of the German people and the emergence of a new democratic Germany with friendly help from our victorious country. From these grand themes to the characterisation of individual episodes and people – it demanded a well-thought-out plan and a very varied musical palette. The work further proved my view that for a composer the cinema is not only a school where he perfects his skill but also a political seminar.[66]

Rarely can any of his statements have included so much whitewash rounded off with such a profound truth. The score has neither a 'well-thought-out plan' nor a 'very varied musical palette', but, in keeping with the times, it *is* a 'political seminar' for the composer as much as the audience.

As so often, the music is used to define the two sides, Soviet and anti-Soviet, with America portrayed through jazz. Jazz in the Soviet Union was in a strange position: popular yet condemned, but, with tacit official approval, reproduced in a Sovietised form. Shostakovich had contributed to the genre without producing anything that was 'jazzy' in any Western sense. However, *Meeting on the Elbe*'s examples are his most convincing, portraying bourgeois and perfidious Americans at play, beating up a black colleague. On-duty soldiers are sardonically given 'Yankee Doodle' as a theme, perhaps intimating that (Southern) racism was endemic in the United States. Though a relatively small part of the film score, Shostakovich had some thoughts on jazz, perhaps feeling that he had to go out of his way to justify having written it at all.[67] Admitting that his jazz had not always been successful, he urged composers to try their hands. Some claimed that it needed a special approach, but light music composer Alexander Tsfasman advised him to orchestrate as he would do normally, and – based on his experience – Shostakovich agreed, before reminding composers of the different make-up of jazz bands (i.e. that a different kind of orchestration is needed). He claimed to have taken 'some pride' in the jazz he had written for the film, but a few years later such music would be completely banned. Jazz musician Alexei Kozlov remembers a saying from the 1950s: 'Today he plays jazz; tomorrow he betrays the nation.'[68] In view of the situation Shostakovich took the precaution of including some songs with texts by Dolmatovsky, and these bolstered his reputation, both at the time and in the mid-1950s when there was a small rash of recordings –

including Paul Robeson singing 'The Song of Peace'. The film also features a third nationality, the Germans, and their town band plays Beethoven's Fifth Symphony, completing the score's set of clichés. Still, even here Shostakovich was able to produce something of interest, and while the arrival of the Russians is unsurprisingly accompanied by Russian-sounding choral music and fanfares, it is prefaced by weird wind-like strings.

This is undoubtedly one of the films that Shostakovich felt least involvement with, and in much of it he was cynically providing what he knew was wanted, at least cost to himself. The ineffectuality of the score is compounded by the music editing, which mixes obviously loud cues at bizarrely low levels and fades down several pieces almost before they have started. Nevertheless, the film (though not the music) won a Stalin Prize – which, again, must have left him with mixed feelings.

With the Seventh Symphony long past, in the depths of the Cold War, Shostakovich's stock in the West fell, and he was name-checked negatively – and in some surprising places. In *I Married a Communist* [USA, 1949] we hear: 'Only one thing bothers me [...] some of these phoney intellectuals and black tie Pinkos. [...] They're worrying about the social significance of the ballet, Picasso's paintings or a Chastakovitch [sic] symphony. [...] There's *work* to be done – NOW – but *not* with a paint brush or a ballet slipper.'[69] On the other side of the divide Arnshtam prepared *The Warmongers* [Podzhigateli voiny] in the late 1940s, and Shostakovich wrote a march for it before it was shelved at the script stage, one of many Soviet films never to get beyond this stage.

The Fall of Berlin [Padenie Berlina]

In the late 1940s the Soviet film industry was instructed to concentrate on a few 'masterpieces'. Production fell to a historic low of between nine and twenty films a year – though few were masterpieces. Despite the events of 1948 Shostakovich was still a favoured film composer, just as he had been at the introduction of sound, but now for different reasons. The composer Vano Muradeli claimed that Shostakovich had been saved only by his work on *The Fall of Berlin*, *The Song of the Forests* and *The Sun Shines Over Our Motherland*, which were written 'on the edge of the abyss to which the Leader had shoved the composer'.[70] *The Fall of Berlin*, Mosfilm's seventieth birthday present to Stalin, was the third of Mikhail Chiaureli's four hymns to the leader the others being *The Great Dawn* [Velikoe zarevo, 1938], *The Vow* [Kliatva, 1946] and *The Unforgettable Year 1919*.[71] Despite single-handedly winning the Great Patriotic War, Stalin still finds time to take a paternalistic interest in the lives of his subjects, though Mikhail Gelovani plays him without moving a muscle, perhaps preferring not to portray him at all for fear of being

War and Cold War (1943–1953) 69

wrong, a fault that marred Boris Shchukin's portrayal of Lenin in other films.[72]

Naturally, the Nazis' shattering of the Soviet idyll brings a chunk of the Seventh Symphony's march, crudely yoking the image not to the music but to its associations, just as silent cinema accompanists had used the 'Marseillaise'. But there are also more reflective moments. Alexei is a Stakhanovite steel worker and soon to be a hero of the Red Army, but he struggles with emotions and worries about his blossoming relationship with schoolteacher Natasha. A touching nocturne takes him to a lake to contemplate the situation. Yet, even at the start of the film, not all seems well, and there are several puzzling moments. Children happily skip through a field, singing Dolmatovsky's verses praising the vernal innocence of the pre-war Soviet Union, while in the background Alexei's factory blackens the sky with infernal smoke. A little later we meet the Great Gardener, tending his garden (filled with red roses) and inspiring awe in Alexei. Almost inaudible is a choir, heavenly and saccharine

11. *The Fall of Berlin*: 'Glory to the Great Stalin', reads the banner; 'Glory to Stalin,' sings the choir

like the one that appeared in *Michurin*; has the baton of Soviet agronomy been passed to Stalin? Alexei tells Natasha about his conversation with Stalin, but is it only retrospectively that the advice – that, if she does not fall in love with him, Alexei should write to Stalin – sounds ominous. As the Soviets overrun Berlin, Hitler marries Eva Braun to the bizarre accompaniment of the Wedding March from Mendelssohn's *A Midsummer Night's Dream*, the last thing Hitler would have been listening to in the bunker. Is Chiaureli mocking the Nazis' inability to recognise the music that they themselves banned or underlining their failure by accompanying this most important ceremony with their most hated music? Or was he simply ignorant of the Nazis' view of the composer? The Nazis were not Chiaureli's only enemy. Mocking Eisenstein, the storming of the Reichstag parodies the famous Odessa steps sequence of *The Battleship Potemkin*. Then Stalin's arrival in Berlin, God-like in white from the skies (an event that never happened), is clearly modelled on Hitler's arrival in Nuremberg in *Triumph of the Will* [Triumph des Willens, Germany, 1934],[73] while, after he has generously acknowledged the contribution of his generals (illustration 11, page 69), the last shot of the film is based on one in the Nazi film *Kolberg* [Germany, 1945].

If these were deliberately Aesopian comments they were not explained by any of the participants, even long after the film's completion. In 1944 Chiaureli told Dovzhenko, 'think what you will, but when you're making a film, you put in what is liked'.[74] The mixture of signs implies that nine years later Chiaureli was hopelessly confused about the film – perhaps simply intoxicated by the almost limitless resources that were available to him. But he seems to have been completely sincere; his actress-daughter Sofiko reports that he was intensely proud when Stalin praised it.[75] Whatever the motives, *The Fall of Berlin* is one of the most fascinating documents of this time, in some ways well made and in others terrible, even ignoring its offensive message.

Together with *The Song of the Forests* it was the closest Shostakovich came to overt praise for Stalin,[76] but he was in no position to avoid it, and most of the blame must lie with Dolmatovsky's texts. He also wrote a miniature two-piano concerto for 'The Storming of the Seelow Heights', but the material is not very memorable, going off at half cock, and the film cuts it into several chunks, further dissipating it. The material was reworked for the second movement of the Tenth Symphony, turning a glorious military engagement into what has been described as 'a gigantic whirlwind overtaking a community'.[77] But he returned to the 'concerto' idea, producing a very enjoyable example for one piano for *The Unforgettable Year 1919*. Shostakovich took no part in the music editing, which is extremely crude, with rapid fades up and down and cuts at painfully inappropriate moments. Ignoring the film, he developed some of its ideas in the Preludes and Fugues and the Tenth Symphony, though both were less hysterically received than the film. He was inspired by the courtship of Ivan and Natasha; she quotes Pushkin to him but he does not recognise it and responds with Mayakovsky. In his 'Four Monologues on Verses by Pushkin' (1952) Shostakovich set the same poem, 'What is My Name to You?', quietly asking to be remembered after death and the following year took some of the music over into his Tenth Symphony.

In 1956 Khrushchev condemned Stalin's personality cult, citing the film and describing the director as 'a wretched little toady', 'totally dependent on Stalin's patronage'; 'after Stalin's death and Beria's arrest we sent him off to the Urals'.[78] Nonetheless Chiaureli continued to direct until his death in 1974. Some of the actors and technicians quietly dropped the film from their biographies. Shostakovich's music, published and recorded, remained visible.[79] Rarely shown for many years, it was restored in the early 1990s, the quintessence of the Stalin personality cult and an example of Soviet kitsch.[80]

Belinsky [Belinskii]

Shostakovich's cinema career continued unsatisfyingly, yet in the face of recent disappointments he put in another plea for libretti for a film-opera, perhaps hoping to take greater control over this aspect of his work.[81] Following the split with Trauberg, Kozintsev was rebuilding his career, and after *Pirogov* turned to another biopic in 1950, this time of the nineteenth-century literary critic Belinsky. But it was 'maimed by insistent demands for never-ending, absurd remakes'[82] and released only in 1953. Shostakovich said little about it in later years, though at the time he described it as one of his most important recent film scores[83] and, as with *Simple People*, assigned it an opus number from the time of composition.

'Reviewing *Belinsky* today, one can hardly believe it was made by a professional, so poor was it.'[84] Admittedly, it would be hard to accord it the status of 'masterpiece' but the film's poverty is largely due to its success in fulfilling all the constraining generic expectations of the Soviet biopic.[85] Stressing Belinsky's importance in the early days of the populist movement, he is portrayed as a liberal member of the intelligentsia, but unlike most of the bourgeoisie he has a feeling for 'the people'. Conforming to Stalin's ideal of excluding the personal aspects of the subjects' lives, as the film progresses it becomes clear that Belinsky, nominally the hero of the film, is actually merely a conduit for *narodnost*. Whenever he is faced with a problem he encounters a group of proletarians or peasants singing a song, even sometimes going as far as to seek them out, to be inspired to overcome the difficulty and return to the job of promoting his favoured writers and populist literature with renewed vigour, taking time out only to advise others to look to the people in the way he did.

For those audience members who still did not get the message, one of the songs is called 'The People's Strength'. At the 1948 musicians' conference Shostakovich and the other composers who came under attack had been accused of writing 'anti-people' music; *narodnost* had become a definition of quality and acceptability, and in response Shostakovich turned to choral music, in *Belinsky* using the folk song collections of Feodosi Rubtsov, with whom he had worked at a Leningrad proletarian theatre in 1932–1933. Shostakovich's other 'folk' pieces from around the time include *The Song of the Forests* (1949), 'Ten Russian Folk Songs' and 'Ten Poems on Texts by Revolutionary Poets' (both 1951), and *The Sun Shines Over the Motherland* (1952). His name appeared over several articles discussing folk music, saying things such as:

> The popular spirit does not mean quoting a folk song; [it] manifests itself in the very nature of the melodies and in how they are developed […]. Finally, the most important criterion is the meaningfulness of the main idea which naturally should be embodied in a highly artistic form.[86]

The overture starts with a broadly flowing theme for strings, that has more than a hint of nobility, but, memorable as it is, it is overused in the rest of the film, turning it almost into a monothematic score. It is used throughout for views of the inspiring Russian landscape, clearly binding both it and the critic to the concept of *narodnost*. When a village comes under attack a clanging version for full orchestra sounds the alarm to alert the people, but Shostakovich's loudly martial music was obviously written before the scene was finished, as some dialogue necessitates it being turned down to allow us to hear. A little later, in the hoariest of clichés, Belinsky thinks about the injustice and the clanging bursts back onto the soundtrack in his head. The overture's second theme, a striking chorale for woodwind deserved to be featured more, and would have brought more variety into the score.

The film is also given a gloss of 'reality' through Belinsky's encounters with Gogol, Turgenev and other literary men of the time, in much the same way that the accuracy of the look-alikes in *The Fall of Berlin* and *The Unforgettable Year 1919* is meant to persuade us of the truth of what we are seeing. But it often simplifies or rewrites history, so that, for instance, Belinsky's subtle differentiation between Lermontov and Pushkin becomes a simple question of 'which one is the more beautiful?' This is hardly surprising, since he thought Pushkin formally superior though with inferior content – a separation of the two qualities that sounds dangerously close to formalism. But it gives Lermontov an opportunity to extol Pushkin and then wax lyrical about all things Russian (ignoring the real Belinsky's Westernising tendencies), whereupon we are transported out of jail to travel across the landscape with a stately choir, later joined by the orchestra, before a title card informs us of the death of Lermontov. While *Belinsky* avoids the 'Hello, Gogol; do you know Turgenev?' school of biopic, it does risk descending into a catalogue of 'great moments in nineteenth-century Russian literature'. One of these is undoubtedly *Dead Souls*, which Belinsky reads while bouncing through the countryside in a carriage, like the novel's hero Chichikov; but, despite this being a favourite novel of Shostakovich's, the music chugs along so anonymously that it seems unsurprising that it is reminiscent of the Twelfth Symphony (1961), generally regarded as one of his poorest.

For Shostakovich, despite his friendship with Kozintsev, *Belinsky* was a work of necessity, and he quickly moved on to other things. Unfortunately, cinematically it was bound to get worse before it got better.

The Unforgettable Year 1919 [Nezabyvaemyi 1919-i god]

The last of Chiaureli's Stalin biographies, *The Unforgettable Year 1919* is as misleading as the others, but it was – naturally – proclaimed a great film in the cinema press. A heavily Sovietised history of a brief period in the Civil War, it includes all the things it should. Stalin is a military genius and endlessly kind to the people, though in reality he spent much of his time in Moscow running the Commissariat of Nationalities. In addition, Lenin had made him People's Commissar of State Control in March 1919, and he was also involved with the Communist International and the eighth Party Congress, leaving little opportunity to leave the city. Britain, France and the United States, embodied in their leaders, are portrayed as rabidly anti-Soviet. Churchill is played by Viktor Stanitsyn, who had also taken the role in *The Fall of Berlin*, but here he is shown not as he looked in 1919 but with the much more recent visage that people would have remembered from the war.

It is one of Shostakovich's most uneven film scores, but it is probably the subject matter as much as this that has dissuaded many people from recording it. Apart from his original material there is a mass of found music in the film, usually with fairly simplistic meanings: the British fleet is accompanied by 'God Save the King' and he finds several opportunities to use, yet again, 'Be Brave Brothers'. A lot of such music is woven into the narrative and is correspondingly fragmentary: someone picking out a few notes on the balalaika. Inverting earlier films' scenes of music masking Bolshevik meetings, here Chopin is used as a cover for the meeting of Polish White supporters, and then later on they dance a polka, frantically hoping to put the Reds off the scent – who are, of course, too clever to be fooled. Much the same happens in St Isaac's Cathedral, where the service and choir's music covers an assignation. Shostakovich also includes a miniature 'piano concerto', 'The Assault on the Red Hill', a title that, misreading 'Shturm krasnoi gorki' as 'Shturm prekrasnoi Gorkii', has often been mistranslated as 'The Attack on the Beautiful City of Gorky'.[87] Yet, despite the title, its first appearance – a two-minute segment – has nothing to do with the Reds' attack on the Whites' fortress, which was on a hill outside Petrograd. Rather, it cuts between Stalin and a group of soldiers, both marching past various Petrograd landmarks, and most notably, as Stalin passes the famous Bronze Horseman statue of Peter the Great, he pauses for a moment to create a tableau: his noble profile in the foreground with his equally visionary predecessor behind him. At the end of *The Fall of Berlin* Stalin's profile is set against the red flag, heralding a new phase in the socialist world. Here the comparison with Peter holds Stalin up, none too subtly, as his equal. When the concerto returns it accompanies the attack proper, yet this sweepingly romantic Rachmaninovian music seems an odd choice for a war scene (illustration 12, below). Despite its inappropriate tone, Shostakovich obviously enjoyed the chance to spread his wings and probably envisaged the images being edited to the music, but Chiaureli frustrated him as, apart from the explosions and gunfire, towards the end the picture cuts to an argument

12. *The Unforgettable Year 1919*: Rachmaninovian music leads the troops into battle

in the trenches, followed by a scene in prison, and the music incongruously has to compete with the shouting and other noises before being abruptly cut off. There is another movement that uses the piano extensively, though less prominently or memorably, and it is further compromised in the film as the recapitulation of the main theme of the overture is almost completely obliterated by shelling.

With such an apparently straight-faced, serious film one might expect a correspondingly heavy score, and that impression is confirmed by Atovmian's suite, yet some moments in the film itself are the nearest thing to Eccentrism without being it. Clémenceau, Lloyd George and Woodrow Wilson are remorselessly mocked; pompous, arrogant and nodding off in meetings, yet hailed by the West. Later, they are found on all fours studying maps like children in a nursery, and Clémenceau stumbles as he mounts the steps in a parody of *Potemkin* that, with its legless man, is even more explicit than *The Fall of Berlin*.[88] Shostakovich joins in the fun, writing a bizarre entrance march that includes an idea he would revisit in *Cheremushki*, followed by one of his most satirically brainless marches, which veers for a few notes into 'God Save the King' (a twisted variation will tell us, later, where the ships in the harbour come from). The film is full of such musical flagging: in a Parisian café the music includes a sequence for balalaikas and one for a gypsy guitarist – normal within Russia but 'exotic elements' in France, and signifying an expatriate haunt where the bourgeoisie sing the 'Tsar's Hymn'; when a soldier is introduced to a meeting, we hear the 'Marseillaise'. Yet this seems to be a case too far; the man is blind, has a shattered arm and is accompanied by two similarly injured comrades – hardly candidates for such glorious music, apart from as an over-the-top anti-war statement.

The Unforgettable Year 1919 in many ways lives up to the adjective. Its distortions of history are one thing and would pass by the ignorant, yet everything about it is grotesque, and it seems sometimes to be being played as a bluntly satirical comedy. Indeed, it is difficult to understand what the audience's reaction would be, with its flawless heroes – an impression compounded by the acting. Lenin visits a construction site that is filled with joyful singing, and happily helps carry logs; Stalin rides the footplate of a train, calmly surveying the scene as bombs explode all about. There is even an attempt to make Stalin more genial, as he arrives at a wedding and cracks a few gags, to the delight of the other guests. But he returns to type, making a serious speech, with choral music in the background. The film climaxes with a meeting between Lenin and Stalin to the blaring overture, which cuts to a train disappearing into the distance, as Stalinism will lead the country into the future.

Chiaureli and Ivan Pyriev were among the chief purveyors of such films (Pyriev's musical *Cossacks of the Kuban* [Kubanskie kazaki, 1950] – 'the most distorted work in Soviet cinema'[89] – notoriously showed joyous farmers producing vast quantities of delicious food). It is difficult to know how they felt about these films. Did they genuinely believe they reflected reality? Were they simply doing such work as was available, trying to ignore moral considerations? Or were they pushing the genre to its limit as a satirical attack? This was partially Eisenstein's hope in *Ivan the Terrible*, but despite Shostakovich's experience in the cinema and his highly attuned sense of humour he missed this, seeing it as a 'distasteful' Stalinist film.[90] Chiaureli does not seem to have been trying to attack the regime satirically. It seems he was flattered by the resources that were made available, and this blinded him to the real content of his films. Shostakovich, wedded to the work only as a way of earning money, was able to stand back and assess the situation more objectively. Yet, despite these high profile commissions, his financial position remained difficult, and when the despised *Song of the Forests* was recorded he quickly enquired about payment through Atovmian, who also helped out by compiling three ballet suites from old scores, including *Michurin* and *The Tale of the Priest*. There was another indirect cinematic near-miss in 1952, when Lewis Milestone considered Shostakovich's Sixth Symphony for the cattle drive in *Kangaroo*, but producer Daryl Zanuck overruled him, apparently not wanting a repeat of the Iron Curtain court case.

After films such as *The Fall of Berlin* and *The Unforgettable Year 1919*, and with production in single figures, Stalinist cinema seemed to have nowhere to go. But it would not be an issue for much longer. On 5 March 1953 Joseph Vissarionich Stalin died.

The country was hurled into turmoil, and there was a power struggle comparable to the one that had followed the death of Lenin (and Russian leaders before him). It was won some time later by Nikita Khrushchev and most decisively lost by NKVD boss Lavrenti Beria, who was shot for treason. But, though Khrushchev is seen as the architect of de-Stalinisation, many things began to be dismantled almost immediately, and the period 1954–1964 is known as 'the Thaw', after a shockingly honest novella by Ilya Ehrenburg, published in the spring 1954 issue of *Novyi mir*. But to see it as a straightforward progression from dark to light is a misunderstanding. Even after Khrushchev's so-called 'secret' speech in 1956, in which he attacked Stalin's 'cult of personality', there was great uncertainty, as waves of liberalisation (e.g. the publication of art critical of the state) were interleaved with more repressions (e.g. events in Hungary).[91] Artists had to stay on their toes to avoid possible repercussions.

5. An Uncertain Thaw (1954–1962): *The Song of the Rivers* to *Cheremushki*

The Song of the Rivers [Das Lied der Ströme]

To date, Shostakovich's original cinema scores had all been for fiction films: Joris Ivens' *The Song of the Rivers* [1954] was his only documentary.[1] Commissioned by the World Federation of Trade Unions (WFTU), it is dedicated 'To the People Who Work On and Around the World's Six Great Rivers', who come together to form a metaphorical seventh river: the international working class converging on the 1953 WFTU Congress in Vienna. Ivens was a respected documentarist, but the Dutch government had revoked his passport for criticising their East India policy and he compiled the film from footage sent by comrades from all over the world. He had an enlightened view of working with composers.

> All the rushes should be shown to the composer before the cutting has actually begun. [...] Although it may seem heresy in the music departments of Hollywood for me to say so, I believe that the composer can be a great help with suggestions for the cutting and timing of the visuals.[2]

Unfortunately, circumstances made this ideal impossible, and, like the images, the soundtrack was assembled from worldwide contributions. After seeing the footage, Shostakovich wrote the music in Moscow, setting texts by Bertolt Brecht translated by Semion Kirsanov,[3] and the orchestra was recorded in Leipzig. Paul Robeson sang the title song in an English translation by Lloyd Brown, though it was only in summer 1954 that he received the invitation, which did not reveal the identities of the composer or lyricist. Ironically, like Ivens, he had no passport at the time, but whereas the director could not enter his homeland the singer could not leave his. The anti-left atmosphere meant he could not find a commercial studio so used his brother's Harlem parsonage with his son acting as engineer. Having been told how long the performance had to last, it fitted the film perfectly but the voice and orchestra do have a slightly different acoustic.[4]

As the footage was silent, the whole soundtrack had to be created, much of it with commentary and some long sections of traditional music. Shostakovich was not expected to score the entire film, but the task may still have been daunting and he boosted his contribution with recycled parts of a dizzying selection of works, such as the series of crescendi from the Eighth Symphony for the H-bomb, and the 'Assault on Red Hill' from *The Unforgettable Year 1919* to warn against German rearmament. The end of the film includes the scherzo from the Tenth Symphony and the finale of the Fifth Symphony (with the reflective middle section cut) for the march to Vienna, before a last choral rendition of the song. Naturally, for the Volga, he reused 'The Song of the Counterplan'. Less naturally, devastated Stalingrad has an echo of the Nazi march from the Seventh Symphony, followed by an anonymous 'glory' march for the rebuilt city.

The film is structured unusually: the conference speeches are not the climax (perhaps, having seen that happen in many Soviet fiction films, they thought it would be too boring) but a middle section that is largely free of music, while the rest of the film is formed of blocks dealing with particular subjects or countries. The music is, similarly, often in large chunks but not wedded to the film's structure, sometimes being simply illustrative and sometimes running over to link one narrative block to the next.

The prelude from *The Return of Maxim*, along with a newly composed title song for a middle section, provides generically 'positive' music for the credits. The song is less than a minute long and identical in each appearance apart from new words, but since it has to serve every river it is also devoid of any local colour, though the Amazon is followed by a variant on flute with an irregular drumbeat; then there is the final peroration.

But some of the original music is among his most interesting, either for itself or for the way it is used in the film. Images of steel works don't get the predictably percussive 'factory music' but a lilting theme on the strings, which are later joined by a fresh (if, in the English version, rather middle-class-sounding) choir. The history of slavery on the Nile brings weirdly probing serpentine woodwind alternating with skittering strings and ancient-sounding hieratic brass. When the commentator says that 'cotton kings still rule Cairo', percussion explodes and the brass roar in rage. Scenes of poverty, hard work, coal picking and scavenging have wandering strings, punctuated by lurching chords that slowly overwhelm the music with a shuddering climax, before, in a didactic sequence cutting between rich and poor, the darkening strings lower and slow and are overtaken by industrial noise as we move back to the factory.

There are also two pieces that are intriguing in another way. An early scene of building works features the brass fanfares that originally hailed Stalin's arrival at the end of *The Fall of Berlin*, while unemployment and inflation, and the resultant strikes, are accompanied by the same film's clanging piano concerto 'Storming the Seelow Heights', though at least here we get to hear more of it than the mangled version in the original. These pieces certainly have the weight necessary for these scenes, but even if he did not want to compose original ones Shostakovich had written any number of fanfares that he could draw on. This and the reuse of the misunderstood Fifth Symphony do imply that Shostakovich was not entirely convinced by the enterprise, though whether it is the film, the WFTU or its internationalist stance is unclear.

Compilation films have a long and honourable tradition (especially for the left wing), but the music can present problems. On one hand some of the cues will be long, apparently giving the composer a greater opportunity to develop the themes, but, following the images, it can become choppy and underdeveloped. Shostakovich was brilliant at handling large structures (five of his symphonies are around an hour long) but for that he needed an autonomy that films denied him; hence, for the more continuous scores, the kaleidoscopic approach of *Alone*. But, while that would have worked with *The Song of the Rivers*, there were practical difficulties. He was not always intimately involved with the films he worked on, but this was an extreme case of arm's-length collaboration, perhaps lowering his level of commitment and making him happy to recycle. This, and the unpopularity of documentary as a genre, has reduced the exposure his music for the film might have had. But he did draft a laudatory article (though it was not published)[5] and wrote to Ivens thanking him for his 'really modest behaviour'.[6]

A prize-winner in the East, the reaction in the West was very different. It was banned in France, and the British Board of Film Censors, claiming to have 'no politics as such', demanded 'one or two' cuts, in fact totalling a third of the film, including the whole of the last two reels.[7] However, an accommodation was reached and the film was shown uncut. It was the first controversial film that Shostakovich had been involved with for some time, but, ironically, he probably knew little if anything of these difficulties. It was probably destined to remain his only documentary; none of his regular collaborators was a great documentarist, and Ivens' later move towards Maoism made collaboration impossible. However, he did take the opportunity once more to extract and arrange the songs as a money earner.[8]

The Gadfly [Ovod]

After a relatively obscure film, Shostakovich's next was a popular success, at least musically. Faintsimmer's *The Gadfly* is based on the English writer Ethel Voynich's novel about a Revolutionary fighting for Italian unification in the 1830s and 1840s. A melodramatic mix of adventure yarn and love story, Voynich's story was immensely popular in the USSR, but it also echoed eternal Soviet concerns: vilifying the Church, binding together several disparate states into a single unit, and the necessity of self-sacrifice for the nation.[9] Once again, Shostakovich saw the chance to extract extra value from his work and signed a contract for a ballet on the same subject, intending to share the music between the two projects. He was going to use the money to buy a new dacha, but then thought better of it and managed to fund it by other means.[10]

Lovers Gemma and Arthur are members of the Revolutionary group Young Italy, but he is tricked into revealing this in the confessional and though this was an accident she breaks with him. Even worse, he discovers that his father is a cardinal. Ashamed, he fakes his own death, before returning as 'the Gadfly', nicknamed for being such an irritant to the authorities. After various adventures he is captured, and urges the unwilling firing squad to shoot. His father rushes in too late. A locket proclaims his undying love for Gemma.

Though *The Gadfly* has themes in common with other films, it also shares some details: Arthur's encouragement of the firing squad echoes any number of noble death scenes (in films from both East and West), for example *Zoya*, and the Revolutionaries left hanging in the street as a warning also has a parallel in that film.

Ironically, Faintsimmer's two most famous films (this and *Lieutenant Kizhe*) are best known for their frequently performed and recorded scores, although both suites are very different from the music as it appears in the films. Shostakovich wrote a lot for *The Gadfly* but parts of it were heavily cut, and in the inevitable suite Atovmian resurrected the unused fragments, though he then imposed major restructurings, combining cues that occur far apart in the film and reorchestrating everything. One of the most notable changes is to orchestrate the organ music. This, obviously, makes it easier to perform the suite in concert or on disc, and he probably had more than half an eye on maximising Shostakovich's royalties. Shostakovich wrote rarely for the instrument and it brought old-fashioned forms to mind (the fugue in *The Golden Mountains* and the passacaglia in *Lady Macbeth*), though it is the religious connotations that make it a natural choice for *The Gadfly*.[11] But Atovmian's orchestration of the service music at the cathedral (as part of the intermezzo) denies us the opportunity to hear Shostakovich's effective, if simple, chorale for the instrument. Moreover, the new colours strip it of the scene's slightly sickly piety, which adds to the irony as Arthur enters the church and looks up at a particularly emaciated Christ – another self-sacrificer. A little later the revelation of his true father's identity brings more organ music, apparently emanating from the crucifix on his desk, and as he picks it up the orchestra takes over for an overwhelming chord before he smashes it to the ground, silencing the music (illustration 13, below). But it is only a pause, and a few seconds later his decision to fake his death to return as a Revolutionary is accompanied by a continuation that brings us back down to earth: righteous anger leading to common sense. The Church, of course, supports the Austrian repression of Italian nationalism, and when a bishop goes to meet the army the orchestra plays a silly little piccolo and side drum march that gradually moves to circle, mindlessly, the trills of the Prelude, opus 87/11: state and church stuck in the same groove.

Atovmian's reorchestrations remove many of the film's colours – ironically, often the 'folk' elements, would be attractive and politically sound (but difficult to reproduce) on the concert platform. Two notable instances are gypsy singing and dancing, used to mask a Revolutionary meeting. A wistful improvisatory piece for two guitars is played by two Revolutionaries at a rebel

13. *The Gadfly*: music shows Arthur the malignancy of religion

camp. In the film this is immediately followed by a bourgeois ball, at which there is a stiffer contredanse and a more free-wheeling but still formal galop. This is one of the most obvious examples of the music expressing class difference – an idea that may have come from Tchaikovsky's *Eugene Onegin*, where the three acts' dance scenes trace Tatiana's progress through society. The orchestra is not entirely excluded from expressing *narodnost*, as a market scene is accompanied by the bustling 'Bazaar' but even here a local musician bursts in momentarily to remind us of 'reality'.

One of the most attractive (if conventional) pieces in Atvomian's suite is the 'Barrel Organ Waltz' but film-goers experienced it completely differently, as part of a complex Ivesian montage of sounds in the town square, mingling with a busking tenor and guitarist and itinerant salesmen. It is an unusually innovative moment, but what could have been a fascinating attempt to use sounds to follow Arthur around the square and get inside his head is rather a random mélange, bearing no relation to his movements.

The great hit was the 'Romance' (actually called 'Youth' in the score). This pained music introduces the sensitive hero in the Cardinal's library, during his political awakening. But it becomes the theme for his and Gemma's relationship, and Atovmian underlines this by inserting a new more passionate middle section, based on 'A Slap in the Face' from her discovery of Arthur's accidental betrayal of the group. A montage of superimposed memories follows *à la Zoya*, while the music struggles upwards and finally breaks through to something like victory as Arthur nears his Revolutionary vocation. All this is underpinned by a ticking clock, making four and a quarter hours of brooding fly by in forty seconds of screen time. When the wounded 'Gadfly' is tended by Gemma she suddenly recognises Arthur and the music veers momentarily into the 'Romance' before turning away as she thinks what to do with this new knowledge. The point having been made, when she confronts him with her suspicion the music does not need to underline the point. However, at the end of the film the cardinal visits Arthur in prison, and there is a recapitulation to bring the story full circle, Arthur calling the cardinal 'padre' with bitter irony. The 'Romance' was later arranged for any number of ensembles, turning up on many compilation discs of Shostakovich's or Russian music, though it took its use as the theme music to the television spy drama *Reilly, Ace of Spies* to bring it wide success in the West.[12] This and a set of other enjoyable character pieces (with occasional nods to the Italian setting) make *The Gadfly* Shostakovich's most popular and frequently recorded film score, though it took a few years to take off. Atovmian compiled the suite in 1955, but it was not published till 1960, and the first recording was released the following year.[13]

The First Echelon [Pervyi eshelon]

The post-Stalin uncertainty seemed to be clearing in 1956, a tumultuous year internationally, nationally and for Shostakovich personally. In February Krushchev's secret speech was a major contribution to de-Stalinisation, though any relief was compromised by later events in Hungary. Personally, the summer brought mixed fortunes. Three years of writing little of importance came to an end with the Sixth String Quartet, he scored Mikhail Kalatozov's *The First Echelon*, and *Simple People* was finally released. In December 1954 his first wife Nina had died, and in 1956 he made a disastrous marriage to Margarita Kainova, who had no conception of his artistic needs, though she was an efficient homemaker. The marriage lasted just three years. He also turned fifty and, though the 1948 decree had yet to be revoked, there were celebrations, and at one a group of Pioneers performed 'The Song of the Counterplan'. Perhaps this spurred him to include it in his operetta *Moscow Cheremushki*, which he began the following year, returning to the song yet again in 1961 to make a version for voice and piano just before the operetta was filmed.

The First Echelon, directed by Kalatozov from a script co-written with Nikolai Pogodin, is about the opening up of Kazakhstan's 'virgin lands' (an alternate title for the film), but it was not Shostakovich's only encounter with the topic; in 1930 he had written music for a stage play on the same theme, and in 1964 he started work on an operatic version of Sholokhov's novel *Quiet Flows the Don*. The long-banned *Simple People* and *The First Echelon* make interesting companions: both are concerned with the group rather than a single hero, and both concern Russians' work in Central Asian republics. They even share an opening setting on-board a train with some light flirting, but, whereas Kozintsev and Trauberg's was essentially a dark vision, Kalatozov and his photographer Sergei Urusevsky fill the journey with light, games and singing. The overture opens with a serious, leaping figure in the strings, like those that had instigated his Fifth, Sixth and Eighth Symphonies, but the mood cannot be sustained, and it quickly softens with the addition of low brass and takes on a youthful striding when the higher instruments enter. Urusevsky was developing his mobile camera technique and 'life caught unawares' style, but, perhaps hindered by unwieldy colour equipment, this is a fairly static affair. However, he manages to move down the carriage as everyone sings the vernal 'Children's Song', bidding farewell to their homes and hello to the steppe. Obviously intended as the 'hit', it recurs throughout the film and was published in the same month that the film was released.[14] Yet elsewhere at the same time an article about film music completely overlooked Shostakovich.[15] Arriving at their destination, the wintry station is filled with welcoming locals dancing in the snow to a series of pieces, including a gentle waltz that Shostakovich reused several times through his career – and reappeared in Kubrick's *Eyes Wide Shut* [USA, 2001]. This gives way to a Soviet march as, laughing uproariously, everyone boards snowploughs to complete the journey.

Kalatozov could never hope to top the mendacity of *Cossacks of the Kuban*, but it is questionable whether he was trying. Pyriev's film and its relentless joy was being questioned, but it was still unclear how much freedom 'the Thaw' would allow. Nevertheless, *The First Echelon* does not shy away from showing difficult working conditions (even if it is only so that they can be overcome) and a range of characters who are not stereotypical – indeed, there are so many that some are under-developed. But this was too much for some, and Party organiser Uzorov was criticised for failing to match up to real Soviet heroes such as Kozintsev and Trauberg's Maxim, and Pavel Korchagin, the hero of Nikolai Ostrovsky's novel *How the Steel was Tempered*.

Unlike Pyriev, Kalatozov includes more reflective moments; some people look forward with trepidation, but Uzorov is on hand to instil confidence, while a guitarist plays a pot-pourri and a girl dances. But, a little later, things get out of hand as the camera moves around the area, picking up sounds like the market square in *The Gadfly*: someone listening to the gramophone, someone playing the guitar and singing, and, in the background, a group practising their song under Uzorov's baton. Naturally, the group wins out, though not after some comic business.

While Pogodin and Kalatozov tried to find the right degree of 'reality' for the film, Shostakovich slipped in his own thoughts unnoticed. The inauguration of a new tractor calls for a celebratory performance by a local rag-tag band: some brass, a cymbal and, naturally, three accordions. But disaster strikes and the tractor gets stuck, while the band uselessly repeat their little fanfare over and over again. Obviously, there is a level of satire in the failed start to the project, and the idiotically repeated music unmistakably underlines that. But Shostakovich goes further by using a fanfare that heralds a speech in *The Counterplan*; apparently, things have not progressed since 1932. Most people would not have recognised it, simply enjoying the stupidity of the tune, but even fewer would realise that he had already reused it once before with a darker implication. In between *The Counterplan* and *The First Echelon* Shostakovich had used the fanfare again, in a piece that almost nobody heard. After the 1948 Musicians' Union conference at which he was denounced Shostakovich wrote a bitter squib mocking the stupidity and ignorance of the main participants, who spout panegyrics about melodiousness, opine that 'anti-people composers can only write anti-people music' and mispronounce Rimsky-Korsakov's name. The text was based on conference speeches and, given that the lead character is clearly Stalin, it obviously could not be made public at the time. Though its existence was long rumoured, it was released only in 1989. Prefaced by a long and hilariously scatological preface, which darkly promises that the authors of the work will be found, much of its history – and even its title – is unclear. Commonly referred to as *Rayok* or *Anti-Formalist Rayok*, the title on the manuscript is *Learner's Manual*.[16] The failure of 1950s agricultural policies is thus linked to the industrial failings of the 1930s, hingeing on Stalin, the source of artistic repression in the 1940s.[17] However, the failure of the tractor cannot be allowed to interfere with the 'virgin lands' policies; it is quickly fixed and, to everyone's delight, ploughs a straight furrow. The band responds appropriately with a rendition of 'The Children's Song'.

Still, there are more difficulties. Petia gets drunk and loses control of a tractor, though it is quickly brought under control, denying the chance of an exciting scene. After being reprimanded he decides to exact revenge: even in 1956 alcoholic wreckers were obviously still a concern. But the raging music has to be turned down for the voices to be audible, and much of it passes for nothing. Of course, there also has to be time for love but everyone seems to be in love with the wrong person; several times, though, we hear a phrase that Shostakovich would reuse for *Cheremushki*'s Masha and Sasha dream of a flat of their own: 'And all the mod cons! Why stand in the hallway? There's a cosy study and the parquet shines like glass.' Very different from their current lives. Despite his position of authority in the kolkhoz, Uzorov does not know how to cope with these matters and goes to a dusky field (just like Alexei in *The Fall of Berlin*), while the celeste picks out a gently falling melody, a near-relative of the song 'The Ninth of January' from his 'Ten Poems on Texts by Revolutionary Poets' (1951): 'Oh Tsar, our little father, look around. Life is impossible because of the Tsar's servants, against whom we are helpless.' This is probably a coincidence, but the *Cheremushki* pre-echo makes sense when the new kolkhoz accommodation is opened (though this is marked with dancing and accordions), before everyone congregates to hear a speech from the kolkhoz manager and watch a play, heralded by the waltz that had welcomed them. But the drunken Petia accidentally sets fire to a wheat field and after watching the end of the play the Komsomol dash to put it out in an exciting sequence that reuses material from the overture and gives Urusevsky his head. At the end of the film a regional official arrives to give a speech, and Uzorov and Ania finally resolve their misunderstanding, while the music rises in a standard climax.

Leningrad Symphony [Leningradskaia Simfoniia]

In 1957, the day after Shostakovich's fifty-first birthday, Zakhar Agranenko's *Leningrad Symphony* opened, a fictional account of the famous work's Leningrad premiere.[18] With the 1948 decree still not revoked this was one of his acceptable works, though the film concentrates on the difficulty of assembling the orchestra and does not portray Shostakovich at all. Apart from the symphonic fragments (played by the Leningrad Philharmonic under Yevgeni Mravinsky on the soundtrack) it was scored by Shostakovich's friend Veniamin Basner. Adding to the film's fiction is the conductor's name, Dobroselsky. Perhaps the concert's real conductor, Karl Eliasberg, sounded too German.

Also in 1957 he completed his Eleventh Symphony ('The Year 1905') but, though it was enthusiastically received at home, criticism in the West centred on its sounding too much like a film score, and comments on it still home in on its pictorialism. But the controversy moved into the political arena when the theory developed that, far from depicting the Bloody Sunday of 1905, it was about the previous year's suppression of the Hungarian uprising. This became a measure of adherence to the 'Shostakovich as dissident' theory, but now there is a measure of balance and it is accepted that it may be about both events, or even political violence in general. However, its 'cinematic' quality, and whether that compromises its symphonism, is still a question that comes up, and it is undeniable that his film scores occasionally draw on the techniques he used in it.

Khovanshchina

Mussorgsky had always been an important composer for Shostakovich but during the war this intensified, and between 1939 and 1941 he produced an edition of *Boris Godunov*, orchestrated 'The Song of the Flea' for *The Adventures of Korzinkina*, and arranged the 'Hopak' for frontline concerts. He returned to the composer in 1962 to orchestrate the 'Songs and Dances of Death' and described his Fourteenth Symphony (1969) as a kind of continuation of that work. Many of Mussorgsky's works are editorial nightmares; he started around nine operas but completed only *Boris Godunov*, and that in two versions; Shostakovich is only one of many who have edited and reorchestrated various works. For many years *Khovanshchina* was known in a completion by Rimsky-Korsakov, and in 1952 Shostakovich had orchestrated some pieces to supplement this for the Kirov Theatre. In 1955, while completing her film of Mussorgsky's *Boris Godunov* (in Rimsky-Korsakov's version), Vera Stroyeva invited Shostakovich to work on a film of *Khovanshchina* as, at around three hours, it needed to be cut for the film. Given his love of Mussorgsky,

Shostakovich naturally accepted and began work even before contracts were signed, deciding that he would continue whether or not the film went ahead and reorchestrate the whole thing rather than just those scenes that would be filmed. But once things had been confirmed he took it up in earnest in 1958, gradually becoming more deeply involved and eventually collaborating on the screenplay. Rather than cut entire scenes he chose often to snip lines and sections to keep the larger structure intact – a different course from the one he would take on the film adaptations of his own *Cheremushki* and *Katerina Izmailova*, which saw more wholesale cuts, additions and revisions. The Bolshoi Theatre considered forbidding the participation of its singers since Mussorgsky's reputation for incompetence made them fear for their voices. However, the arrival of the score reassured them (eventually) and they went ahead with the filming.

Mussorgsky was fascinated by history, and his two greatest operas had a contemporary resonance. Writing to his librettist Vladimir Stasov about *Khovanshchina*, he repeatedly stressed: '*We haven't moved!* [...] The past within the present – that is my task.' While Peter the Great's efforts to claim the throne and the sentencing of the 'Old Believers' to death did not have a direct parallel in the 1870s, the continued oppression of the people was more what Mussorgsky had in mind. The parallels with the mid-1950s are more interesting. The Old Believers could be shadows of the Stalinists who were being eased out, but, paralleling Mussorgsky's feelings, it is the unchanging situation that Stroyeva and Shostakovich regret rather than the passing of this or that regime. However, the opera's relevance was lessened by 1959, when it reached the screen.

In the 1960s song scores enjoyed another wave of popularity with the rise of a new generation of composers. But Shostakovich stayed away from the technique. The poets and lyricists of the Thaw were not of his generation and Yevtushenko was the only one he worked with. He and many of his contemporaries held faith with the symphonic score while others experimented with song or increasingly complex soundscapes or electronic scores made possible by Yevgeny Murzin's invention in the late 1950s of the ANS, a unique instrument named after Alexander Nikolaevich Skriabin.

By the early 1960s the deterioration in Shostakovich's health was growing increasingly apparent; his weakening right hand left him unable to play the piano in public, and eventually he had to train himself to write with his left. Nevertheless, he continued to work on films, though he did slow down, in his last fifteen years working on only seven more films. But, though there were fewer of them, they were often more important to him. Five were works by close friends, while the other two were adaptations of his stage works: *Cheremushki* [1962] and *Katerina Izmailova* (the revised *Lady Macbeth of Mtsensk*, 1967); Arnshtam's *Five Days, Five Nights* [1961] and *Sofia Perovskaia* [1968];

Kozintsev's *Hamlet* [1964] and *King Lear* [1970]; and Grigori Roshal's *A Year is Like a Lifetime* [1965], loosely based on Galina Serebriakova's biographical novel about Marx. Of these, *Katerina* and Kozintsev's films were the most important to him. His existing music was also increasingly being used in films, such as the 1967 anniversary release of Eisenstein's *October*, but the composer took little or no part in these.[19]

Outside his film work he was beginning to write pieces that more outspokenly addressed the country's problems or countered the still-dominant Socialist Realism, notably in the Thirteenth and Fourteenth Symphonies (1962 and 1969) and *The Execution of Stepan Razin* (1964).[20] Where in the middle of his cinema career, there had been a divergence between his film and concert music, the former often being politically compromised, from the mid-1960s onwards the films began to engage on a different political level, and one more in tune with Shostakovich's own feelings.

Five Days, Five Nights [Piat' dnei, piat' nochei]

In July 1960 Shostakovich visited Dresden in connection with Lev Arnshtam's film *Five Days, Five Nights*, a Soviet-East-German co-production.[21] So moved was he by the still not fully reconstructed Dresden that, as well as writing the film score, he composed his Eighth String Quartet 'In Memory of the Victims of Fascism and War' in the space of three days. Or so went the Soviet story, ignoring the fact that Shostakovich had visited the city a decade earlier without writing such a piece. It also ignored the very pointed quotations from his own works that litter the piece, identifying a very particular victim, as he had been informed that he was expected to join the Communist Party – something that he had so far avoided.[22] One response to his problems was to consider, not for the first time, suicide, intending the quartet as his own requiem. But he was dissuaded from killing himself.[23] He finally signed his Party membership in October 1961. In 1992 Maxim described it as one of the only two times he saw his father cry.[24] The quartet includes the four-note 'march to death' from *The Young Guard*, but hearing it in the context of the film is even more striking. Before killing the youths the Nazis tell Komsomol members to step forward. One hangs back and is asked: 'Are you not a Party member?', whereupon we hear the motif. With this quote Shostakovich ironically aligns himself with the Young Guard, who die for being members of the Party; for him, membership of the Party was a moral death. No one who has seen the film and knows the quartet could miss this, though after twelve years he probably felt safe in making the connection.

Back on cinema duty, by 19 July 1960 Shostakovich had seen *Five Days*, and he wrote to Glikman, 'Much of it gives me great pleasure. Lyola's

[Arnshtam's] goodness of heart absolutely shines through it, and that is the main quality of his film.'[25]

Five Days, Five Nights tells the exaggerated story of how Russian and German troops collaborated to save art works in post-war Dresden. It includes many of the expected elements: children being rescued, self-sacrifice, friendly collaboration between (certain) nations, and the preservation of culture (a kind of fictional counterpart of the *kino-kontsert* films). But, apart from immensely boosting the Soviet role, Arnshtam had to work hard to inject some excitement. In the end the genial Sergeant Kozlov, beloved by all the children, is killed when he finds a booby-trapped cache of paintings – further evidence of the Nazis' cynical philistinism. Arnshtam also wound into the film the love story between Paul, a one-armed painter, and Katrin, a concentration camp survivor. According to Arnshtam:

> Saving the paintings of the Dresden Gallery is not the main topic of this film. The meaning of real humanism is the fight for the heart and the spirit of man himself. [...] I want to emphasise how wonderful it was to collaborate with my colleagues at DEFA. [...] I am absolutely sure that I found new friends in the GDR.[26]

But neither he nor Shostakovich seemed particularly inspired by the events. After slow-moving, stately credit music, the long pan over Dresden's ruins that opens the story is accompanied by high, trembling strings and fragmentary fanfares on muted trumpet, inevitably bringing to mind the Eleventh Symphony, though the parallel between Dresden in 1945 and St Petersburg in 1905 is hazy at best. Perhaps Shostakovich is hinting that both saw the destruction of a culture. But it takes a Soviet to see the value of Dresden's art and organise its rescue: Rembrandt's *Self Portrait with Saskia on his Knee* is covered so thickly with dust that it is invisible until he brushes it off, almost as if he knew what was underneath.[27] And, in case we do not understand what we are seeing, characters occasionally explain with their fellows standing in for us. But, though the Soviets are saving the museum, German culture cannot be entirely ignored, and when two former fellow soldiers meet, the music seems familiar but is just out of the grasp of our memories. Slowly it coalesces and suddenly snaps into focus: the main theme from the finale of Beethoven's Ninth Symphony, the *Ode to Joy*, the embodiment of the humanism of which Arnshtam spoke.[28] This process of revelation recurs in the restoration of the paintings, the city and the friendly pre-war relations, and when Paul and Katrin meet they only slowly recognise each other, as a high, thin flute wanders over tremulous strings before a sinking clarinet line warms the music; she looks at his painting, and the love theme emerges. Paul himself struggles with the mental aftermath of losing his arm, and slowly comes to terms with the Soviets.

This is one of Shostakovich's most colourful film scores for some time: when Katrin and Paul wander around the city ruins with some children they are accompanied by a light, Vaughan-Williams-ish pastorale for oboe and pizzicato strings that, differently orchestrated and a notch or two faster, would have fitted perfectly into *Cheremushki*. In another sequence a restorer walks through the collection to probing, darkly wandering strings that, after three attempts, manage to get to their feet.[29] With scenes of the army mobilising, the music moves into a pizzicato march punctuated by brass fragments, before returning to the initial music.

Unsurprisingly, all the art on display is traditional and representational but this presents a potential problem: the old masters' liking for religious subjects. But their status as 'humanist-artists' overrides any religious content and Raphael's *Sistine Madonna* is given a special guard, as well as some mildly Vivaldian music (though with the odd addition of an occasional tam-tam) the oscillations of which slowly become more Shostakovichian, redolent of works such as the Second Violin Concerto (1967) and the Twelfth String Quartet (1968).

The film ends with reconciliations and yet another superimposition. Following Kozlov's funeral, the previously aloof Paul begins to develop a friendship with the children who had so loved him, and the oboe pastorale returns, its similarity to Kozlov's music linking soldier and artist, Soviet and German. And then, at the climax, one of the children's faces is superimposed on marching soldiers, but the music, unlike *Zoya*, is less glorious, perhaps questioning the outcome.

Once again, in compiling the suite, Atovmian removed the organ part (a quiet processional in church and a sort of mini-concerto, less baroque than in *The Golden Mountains*), but *Five Days* is one of Shostakovich's least regarded film suites, perhaps the regurgitated Beethoven throwing its originality into question.

Cheremushki

The stage premiere of the musical comedy *Moscow Cheremushki* in 1959 brought several articles under Shostakovich's name.[30] Officially he had 'worked on the operetta with great enthusiasm', and hoped it would not be his last. It 'touches in a gay, dynamic form on the vital question of the house-building programme', to make a 'jolly and lively show' where 'now and again I parody elements from music that used to be popular not long ago and quote some songs by Soviet composers'. Cheremushki is a large housing estate to the south-west of Moscow named after the bird cherry tree *prunus padus* which was a common sight on such estates and is the species to which Michurin compares his daughter in the 1949 film.

Shostakovich certainly liked operettas, but in private he was less enthusiastic about *Cheremushki*, written as a favour to the Moscow Operetta Theatre's

Grigori Stoliarov, director of the production of *Lady Macbeth* that had enraged Stalin. Nevertheless his professional pride led him to rewrite several songs to make the show as effective as possible. But after attending the rehearsals Shostakovich wrote that he was 'burning with shame' over this 'boring, unimaginative, stupid' piece.[31] Despite this warning, a couple of years later Glikman suggested that Gerbert Rappaport direct a film version. Glikman cut some of the 'slangy' dialogue, and somewhat unwillingly Shostakovich wrote a couple of new pieces,[32] though he came to prefer it to the stage version for the effectiveness of the fantasy sequences.[33] One unexpected outcome was meeting Irina Supinskaia, one of the editorial team for its publication, later to become his third wife.

In the slightly more relaxed atmosphere Vladimir Mass and Mikhail Chervinsky, *Cheremushki*'s librettists, had taken the opportunity to criticise gently local Party officials in the same way as films such as *Carnival Night* [Karnaval'naia noch'] and *The Cranes are Flying* [Letiat zhuravli] [both 1957]

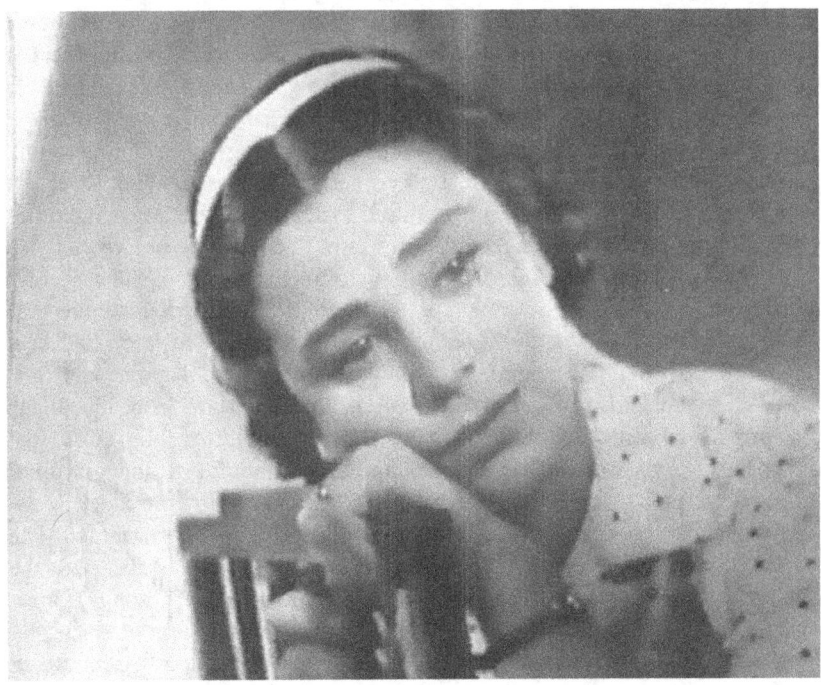

14. *Cheremushki*: 'I live all alone, always alone, like dry land surrounded by water' – A momentary sadness

had done, but between the stage premiere in 1959 and the release of the film in 1962 a new reality was setting in, and the finale was changed to remove the observation that *Cheremushki* itself is a sugary view of Soviet life. Western producers misunderstood it: an operetta about moving into a new flat, and featuring a female construction worker, probably made them think of grey Socialist Realism, and the few who took the trouble to look at the music would have seen it as simply banal. As a result it was largely overlooked, and, though the film was released in the USA under the title *Song Over Moscow*, its British stage premiere took place only in 1994.[34] The original demanded musical forces and stage facilities equivalent in the West to a full-scale opera house but which were available to the many Soviet operetta companies, as the genre was immensely popular. As Gerard McBurney notes, 'There is after all something intrinsically hilarious about silly tunes, not to mention the soap opera-like passions of the characters, being belted out by or over a large symphony orchestra'.[35]

Shostakovich added to these comic effects with a patchwork of quotes from other pieces, including Tchaikovsky's Sixth Symphony and *Swan Lake* and Solovev-Sedoi's worldwide hit *Midnight in Moscow*. Some of these quotes came from the most bizarre sources. The Act One pantomime includes one of the dances from *The Great Citizen*, here made to accompany a dream sequence of dancing furniture; perhaps it was a kind of exorcism to find a less repellent use for a good tune. He also yet again reused 'The Song of the Counterplan', this time setting Lidochka's lament about her lovelessness: 'When I went to school, I remember in the evenings, I used to study, study, study, sometimes long into the night.' A long list of topics follows before the pointed pay-off line: 'And that an island is dry land surrounded by water.' The second section makes her desires even more explicit: 'What to say to make him understand that I am ready to share a nest ... but I live all alone, always alone, like dry land surrounded by water' (illustration 14, page 91). But, despite the sadness of this lyric, at the end of the song Lidochka's face lights up, proving that no Soviet citizen can be downhearted for long. Finally, it reappears in Act Two, when the 'lovers' agree to part, but, in a slow variation, they both regret that they cannot get the other to see how they feel. More intriguingly, to mock the corrupt petty officials Shostakovich combined 'The Dance of the Bureaucrats' from the long-forgotten ballet *The Bolt* with the fanfare he had already used against *The Counterplan*'s speechifying, against *Rayok*'s Stalin and against *The First Echelon*'s virgin lands programme. By now it seems to have expanded to become a general theme for Soviet bureaucratic stupidity.

Just as the role and nature of love had come under scrutiny in the 1930s so the Thaw brought a comparable situation. In *The Lesson of Life* [Urok zhizni,

1957, released in Britain as *The Wife*] Natasha decides to stay in an unsatisfying marriage. Though the times and the context may have changed, Lidochka was struggling with similar questions, looking not for something revolutionary but for a traditional relationship.

Everyone in the audience would have spotted the song but may not have considered the ambiguity. At its simplest level it allows people to enjoy the return of an old friend. But, beyond that, it compares Soviet love in the 1930s and the 1950s – and in a strangely conservative way considering that, despite Shostakovich's own first marriage being extremely close, both partners had affairs, reflecting the sexual casualness of the time. Finally, at a third level, the construction of *Cheremushki*, like *The Counterplan*, proposed an ambitious plan, and one that is achieved only through fiddling the figures, with the song linking the two times. 'The Song of the Counterplan' had been a hit in the 1930s and now was 'virtually Khrushchev's theme tune',[36] though, ironically, the estate itself spent some time being named after Brezhnev. Nevertheless, Cheremushki still (just about) stands – an indictment of a failed housing policy.

Ironically, while Shostakovich was producing one of his lightest scores, an older, darker one was contributing to Polish director Andrzej Wajda's *Siberian Lady Macbeth* [Sibirska Ledi Magbet, 1962]. This was yet another version of Leskov's story, in which the few fragments of music were drawn from Shostakovich's opera, though the composer was not involved.

6. Endgame (1964–1975): *Hamlet* to *King Lear*

Hamlet [Gamlet]

Russia had known Shakespeare since the eighteenth century, with its discovery of romantics such as Byron, with whom the playwright was grouped. 'Westernisers' furthered this agenda, and in the nineteenth century he became a cult figure, inspiring many artists and making 'Shakespearean' a critical term; David Oistrakh used it to describe the solo part of Shostakovich's First Violin Concerto (1948). In the twentieth century Lenin's admiration for him may have given his reputation a (hardly needed) boost. Writers of such widely varying talent as Catherine the Great and Pushkin saw Shakespeare's work as a model for drama, and many others used various plays as templates, reference points or items for study, including Leskov's *Lady Macbeth of Mtsensk* (1865), Turgenev's *A Prince Hamlet of the Schigrov District* (1854), *Hamlet and Don Quixote* (1860) and *A King Lear of the Steppe* (1870), Chekhov's *The Seagull* (1896) and Pasternak's *Dr Zhivago* (1955). Musicians were also inspired to write orchestral pieces, operas or music for theatrical productions, leading to Balakirev's *King Lear* (1858–1861, revised 1902–1905) and Tchaikovsky's *Romeo and Juliet* (1869–1880), *The Tempest* (1873) and *Hamlet* (1869–1880), while there have been innumerable settings of sonnets. 'Hamletism', a chronic inability to act, and its home-grown equivalent 'Oblomovism', after the indolent hero of Goncharov's 1859 novel, became recognised types of behaviour, and the Decree on the Film *A Great Life* accused *Ivan the Terrible* of turning the Tsar into 'a Hamlet figure'.[1]

The accusation was also laid at Shostakovich's door, and his Fifth Symphony was sometimes called his '*Hamlet Symphony*', but he shared the love and completed or considered many Shakespeare projects. He tackled *Hamlet* three times: Akimov's notorious 'comic' version in 1932, and twice with Kozintsev – a 1954 staging that used music largely drawn from their 1941 *King Lear*, and the 1964 film. He was due to write the music for Kozintsev's 1943 staging of *Othello* though in the end he did not. However, in that year he did set Sonnet 66, 'Tir'd with all these, for restful death I cry', reorchestrating it in 1971.[2] The first of the 'Seven Romances on Poems of Alexander Blok' (1967) is 'The Song of Ophelia' and in 1974 he set 'Hamlet's Dialogue with his Conscience' as one of the Tsvetaeva songs. There were also some non-starters, including asking Glikman for a libretto on any play apart from *Othello*, and, most tantalisingly, Meyerhold's suggestion of an operatic *Hamlet*.

Kozintsev had also studied the playwright since proposing *Hamlet* as a FEKS project in the 1920s. His vision was grimmer than Akimov's, and, though some may see comments on the dying days of Khrushchev's rule (he was ousted in late 1964), he had been planning the film for several years; Kozintsev stressed its contemporaneity ('We are not in a museum but facing the conflicts of modern man'),[3] but relating it to specific events narrows its relevance. It is a severe view of the Soviet Union of the time, with its struggles for supremacy and the questionable validity and viability of the rulers. In his late work Kozintsev drew on the theories of stage director Gordon Craig, paring the visuals down to an elemental level ('stone, iron, fire, earth and sea'),[4] and also painter and stage designer Alexander Tyshler a fellow-pupil of Alexander Exter.[5] All this chimed with Shostakovich's increasing reliance upon simple gestures.

Shostakovich was keen to collaborate, but his progress reports were contradictory. After accepting the commission in early 1962, he claimed to have almost finished the music in October.[6] But, interviewed on radio in September 1963,[7] he was 'about to start work', and in October said that *Hamlet* and *A Year is Like a Lifetime* (under the working title *Karl Marx*) 'await my attention (I have seen some of the first sequences for *Hamlet* and they seem to be excellent). These are important pictures and will naturally require a lot of serious thought.'[8] Test shots of Smoktunovsky in the lead amounted to most of his part,[9] so Shostakovich may have been writing music based on this. He wrote most of the music in Moscow and Leningrad, finishing it off in Gorky in early 1964 while attending a festival of his music, and one of the concerts included some excerpts – a rare example of his film music being heard first in the concert hall. Again, he considered an offshoot work, a symphonic poem, but his enthusiasm rapidly died back and he turned instead to his unrelated Ninth String Quartet.[10]

Discussing his Thirteenth Symphony (1962), which sets five poems by Yevtushenko, Shostakovich spoke of 'the problem of civic, repeat, civic morality,'[11] and Kozintsev revealed that Hamlet's encounter with the ghost embodies 'the noble theme of social duty'.[12] In his late, uncompromising works Shostakovich became increasingly concerned with leadership, conscience and honour, and musical themes also recur from work to work. The lashing chords that at the start of the film accompany a close-up of Elsinore's rocks are echoed in 'Creativity' from his 'Suite on Verses of Michelangelo' (1974), and the poet's claim that without the guiding hand of God he is nothing is reminiscent of Hamlet's helplessness. But the non-film work that is closest to *Hamlet* is the Thirteenth Symphony, and there is a musical link to its the third movement, 'In the Store', which describes a queue of women in a shop, and contemplates their suffering and enormous contribution to the country. 'To short-change them is shameful, to give them short measure is sinful' is followed by a series of sharp whip-crack chords, after which he adds: 'As I shove dumplings into my pocket I sternly and silently observe their pious hands, exhausted from carrying shopping.' These chords also occur in the film, very quietly underlining 'The rest is silence'; is Shostakovich implying that Hamlet would short-change the women? Or that sufferers of Hamletism will fail to defend them? Even the structure of the symphony's first movement is cinematic, though this is in part due to the rapid scene changes in Yevtushenko's text, which Shostakovich unmistakably marks off with his music. In turn, the film score is one of his most symphonic, with clever and illuminating developments of the various themes.

One of the few pieces of source music in the film is the court fanfare, beginning with a blackly humorous constipated alternation of two notes. But in the final scenes it begins to dominate more and expands its melodic outline, pointedly appearing as Claudius poisons Hamlet's drink, just as he poisoned the king and with him the Danish court, and, as Gertrude drinks it, reminding us of her role in the tragedy. The duel scene also hints at the end of the Eleventh Symphony, a work that deals with the fall of another rotten court, the Romanovs. But the film ends as it began, with images of the sea and rocks and the music of Hamlet, whose ineffectuality has endangered the state.

Earlier film scores had often had to contrast Soviet and anti-Soviet, but in *Hamlet* the major contrast is between masculine and feminine; Hamlet father and son, and Ophelia. Hamlet's theme thrusts and stabs, often in the brass, but is just as likely (as in 'To be or not to be') to appear on low woodwind before rising up and evaporating. The theme occurs several times in Hamlet's absence, reminding us of his dilemma or other people's relationship to him – as, for example, when a fleeting shadow of it follows the more 'Ophelian' music as she contemplates his picture. However, Hamlet's monologues do not automatically use his theme, and for 'How weary, stale, flat and unprofitable' we hear the lively music that surrounds Hamlet, contrasting with his inner mood in the same way that image and music had conveyed separate messages in *New Babylon*.

Rather than accompanying the ghost with quiet, eerie music Shostakovich provides a full-on brass and percussion chorale-fanfare, underlining his grandeur and the terror he instils, with his wind-whipped black cape against the black sky (filmed in slow motion), moving the encounter to a 'time out of joint'. The clock even plays his theme, making him an eternal presence in the castle. It also returns at crucial moments; as Hamlet attacks his mother it bursts onto the soundtrack (and into his head) to remind him of his promise to leave her for his father to deal with, and we hear it when the ghost finally goads Hamlet into action ('Venom, do your work'). There are also echoes of it both as Claudius wrestles with his own conscience and during *The Mousetrap* (despite Hamlet's claim that the play 'touches us not'). This static scene contrasts with the lively music until the very end, when it is as if the music has finally forced the pictures into activity.

Ophelia is portrayed by gentler, more continuous melodies and delicate instrumental colours, particularly the harpsichord, which haltingly accompanies her music lesson, mechanically echoes her transformation into a marionette as she is strapped into a stiffly corseted dress, and – like a broken clock struggling to maintain time – follows her descent into madness.[13] But, as perfect as this timbre seems, Kozintsev and Shostakovich initially thought of violin with piano or guitar, and then violin alone.[14] When she distractedly re-enters the court the harpsichord alternates with chorale-like strings – a 'call and response' gesture that Shostakovich used in later works, including 'The Death of the Poet' from the Fourteenth Symphony, 'Night' from the Michelangelo Suite and, featuring the cello, the Fifteenth Symphony. The chorale also alternates with tapping timpani, and, appropriately, he would use the same gesture in setting Tsvetaeva's 'Hamlet's Dialogue with his Conscience' (1974). Finally, we go to the river, where Ophelia lies in the water as in Millais' painting,[15] and then to the coast, where her soul, in the form of a gull, flies over the bay to a fluttering flute and oscillating figures like those in the Second Cello Concerto (1967) and Twelfth String Quartet (1968).

The arrival of the actors brings suitably carnivalesque music, and Shostakovich repeats a trick from his 1932 *Hamlet* by scoring another 'orchestral tuning up' sequence, but though in the stage version this had gone on at excruciatingly hilarious length here it is cut to more realistic proportions. Another scene that was important to both director and composer was the one where Hamlet talks about being played like a flute, and *Testimony* discusses it in a lengthy section about Shakespeare.[16] In Akimov's production the prince had put the flute to his anus and 'played' Davidenko's proletarian song 'They Wanted to Beat Us' but Kozintsev, far removed from the spirit of FEKS plays the scene straight.

Between the war and his death in 1973 Kozintsev made only five films. After the disappointments of *Pirogov* and *Belinsky* came three literary adaptations. *Don Quixote* [Don Kikhot, 1957] began his career's recovery, and *Hamlet* saw the international renaissance, but he would complete just one more film: *King Lear*. Kozintsev and Smoktunovsky won Lenin Prizes, a 1966 stamp celebrated the film and Shostakovich was very happy with it; after going to see it eight or nine times, he wrote congratulating Kozintsev.[17] For once the score attracted press comment both at home and abroad, winning an award for best film music at an all-union film festival before being used for several *Hamlet* ballets; overturning the usual interest in concert over film music, *Stepan Razin* has been relatively ignored compared to it.

A Year is Like a Lifetime [God kak zhizn']

Hamlet was a dominating literary figure in Shostakovich's life but Karl Marx was a dominant political figure in the lives of everyone in the USSR. Perhaps this is why it took so long for a biographical film to be made. The cancellation of Kozintsev and Trauberg's 1940 film left Grigori Roshal's 1965 film as the first in-depth Soviet dramatisation of its philosophical father's life. Roshal was well versed in the genre, having made *Academician Ivan Pavlov* [Akademik Ivan Pavlov, 1949], *Mussorgsky* [1950] and *Rimsky-Korsakov* [1952]. Galina Serebriakova co-wrote the script, based on her own novel, and asked him to write the score. Her many years in the camps had not diminished her faith in Marxism, and the film is incredibly earnest, bogged down in its own seriousness. As with earlier Soviet biopics the hero has no life outside his one-dimensional contribution to Soviet history, in this case publishing the 'Communist Manifesto' and the *Neue Rheinische Zeitung* at the risk of imprisonment, and being deported from Belgium, Germany and France. If Shostakovich was inspired by the film he found it difficult to start work on it, and he complained to Glikman on 23 April 1965: 'Evidently I am coming to the end of the road as a composer. I simply cannot write the music to the Karl Marx film. Roshal is furious with me.'[18] However, by 19 June he had 'got through the drudgery of writing the score for Karl Marx', and it was recorded on 21 June. 'The number of leaves added to my crown of laurels as a result of this work will be, I fear, small.'[19] He may have suffered Roshal's ire but he wrote little of anything that year, as, in between, illness he oversaw stagings of *Katerina Izmailova* and began work on the film version.

The strain showed. Starting with a conventional march in his 1930s style we are next treated to both the 'Marseillaise' and 'Ça ira', two Revolutionary songs that he had used in *New Babylon*, but this time as a simple indicator of 'Revolutionary times'. Momentarily the music moves out of his 'Soviet heroic' mode, replaced by grotesquely squealing woodwind and clicking percussion when a young man entertains a crowd with a shadow play, before enthusing them with a cry of 'Hail the Revolution!'. Immediately afterwards, we move to the town square, where, for no apparent reason, the police move in to break up a crowd, to swirling strings and leaping brass. They move on to Marx's house and he is arrested, spending some time in a cell with a violent prisoner, and crystallising some of his ideas on economic slavery. But the violence is only on the screen; we hear a tiptoe pizzicato march.

The music for the film is almost all 'external', either being part of the narrative or describing events and atmospheres, and only touching states of mind when they are themselves reflected by the mise en scène, as when Jenny Marx runs through the rain to trembling strings. At a fair, two clowns echo the plot of *Petrushka*, comically fighting over a girl (accompanied by a violin that out-sentimentalises *The Gadfly*) before a general dancing scene that weirdly begins with the fanfare that opens the First Jazz Suite's polka before embarking on a loose-limbed dance – one of several such sequences. One of the film's few effective cues comes when we move to Germany, where the music for a battle combines gestures from (though not quotations of) both the Eighth and Tenth Symphonies, with the post-battle scene ironically accompanied by wistful pizzicato and woodwind before a winding clarinet introduces darker chiming bells and hollow strings. Shostakovich's contribution is the least of his later films, and since so much of it is simply part of the narrative, large parts are subsumed beneath the dialogue. However, it was the last time that he would be involved in such an unsatisfying cinema project.

Katerina Izmailova

Shostakovich had 'looked again' at *Lady Macbeth of Mtsensk* in March 1955, just three months after the death of his first wife, Nina – its dedicatee. A couple of years later he told friends that he had finished it, but it was still not rehabilitated and plans for productions came and went before the stage premiere in 1963, when it was known as *Katerina Izmailova*. The next year he insisted that La Scala perform that rather than the original. Glikman helped tone down parts of the libretto, including changing Katerina's explicit sexual fantasies to thoughts of cooing doves. Meanwhile, Shostakovich revisited the music, with the most famous change being the removal of the trombones' detumescent glissandi.[20] But he also composed replacement interludes and made the vocal line easier to sing. The Kiev production was Shostakovich's favourite, and they were invited to record the soundtrack for Mikhail Shapiro's film version. Like many opera films it cuts the original work, shoots on location rather than the studio and has actors mime to existing recording – except for Vishnevskaya, who both sings and acts. Sadly the soundtrack recording has never been commercially released, since, even in this abbreviated version, it is a fascinating comparison with her later recording of the original version.[21] As well as overseeing Glikman's revision to the screenplay Shostakovich took charge of editing the music, and apart from rewriting the interludes he cut the whole of the scene in which the police brag about their corruption. It had not lost its relevance over the previous thirty years but it is the most obvious candidate for removal, taking us away from the heroes, even if only for ten minutes.[22] *Katerina Izmailova* is a more innovative film than most opera films of the time, using split screens and superimpositions, though, admittedly, in a rather pedestrian fashion: for instance when the peasant runs to report Izmailov's murder to the police the screen is split diagonally, while Katerina's daydreams are brought to life through superimpositions.

It was the closest he would come to his idea of film-opera and after initial apprehension expressed his satisfaction with the result; ('the film was fine').[23] However Vishnevskaya was critical of the sound balance,[24] a view with which *Testimony* agrees.[25] Egorova implies that an artificial stereo track was generated from the original mono.[26]

The Young Girl and the Hooligan [Devushka i khuligan]

At about the same time another cinematic adaptation of a theatre piece was mooted, though Shostakovich was far less enthusiastic about Ilya Kiselev's *The Young Girl and the Hooligan*. This short ballet, based on a Mayakovsky film script, was compiled by Atovmian from various old scores, including the 'Romance' from *The Gadfly*, and was topped and tailed with 'The Death of the Old Worker' from *The Vyborg Side*. Shostakovich dismissed it as a ballet, and his involvement in the film stopped at giving his permission. Also around this time a documentary about the composer was planned, but the script did not meet with his approval, and he ironically used Soviet officialese to criticise it for not giving sufficient weight to the events of 1948. Glikman and Khachaturian agreed with him, but the studio refused to change the script after an impasse, and the film was not made.[27]

Sofia Perovskaia

The fiftieth anniversary of the Revolution was a great event and one of the celebratory contributions was Arnshtam's *Sofia Perovskaia*. The daughter of St Petersburg's Governor-General, she rebelled against her stultifying bourgeois upbringing to join the Revolutionary movement the People's Will, and was executed for her part in the assassination of Alexander II in 1881. Continuing to stress *narodnost*, the film's publicity said that, 'Her strength lay in the deep consciousness of her duty to the oppressed people. Her weakness was that she did not know and understand the genuine laws of social development, the ways and means of fighting for the happiness of the people.'[28]

Sadly, Arnshtam's wife died during pre-production, and, though Shostakovich himself was in hospital, he still agreed to write the score. However, with no chance to see the film he had to base it on the script and Arnshtam's timings for each section, and – again – he chose to produce a large number of fragments, presumably so that the production team could shuffle them around in post-production. Curiously, he had considered the heroine as the second subject in the planned tetralogy of operas that began with *Lady Macbeth*, and scoring the film, despite being at a distance, was more than a money-earning favour to a friend. Though a clichéd story, Shostakovich produced one of his most original scores: for instance, while the piccolo is an obvious symbol of the militia, it joins the side drum with a banal skittery melody like something from his early theatre scores. The credits' overture follows the broad arc of the narrative formed from this, seguing into the 'Tsar's Hymn', and then into the clanging of bells – perhaps representing the public announcement of the assassination – before the march's return.

Arnshtam gave this martyrology a slightly more complex structure than *Zoya*'s, starting by following Sofia down the street subtly acknowledging other members of the group on her way to the assassination. But she is a mysterious character, who will only slowly be revealed through flashbacks during her interrogation and trial, and at the beginning we do not see her face; when she turns, the camera drops to watch her take a pistol from her coat. Meanwhile, timpani roll like thunder and military fanfares are wrenched upwards to increase the tension. The timpani return when we finally see her face, though her expression is not so much quiet determination as zombified single-mindedness, in common with her bomber colleague. Following the explosion is one of the most extraordinary cues that Shostakovich ever wrote; redolent of his late string quartets, especially the Twelfth (the next piece he wrote) and Thirteenth, it is dissonant, slowly curdling and ending like a cliff edge. But the film also features gentler music, and after a revelatory encounter with the poor of the city she embarks on good works, the trembling strings evoking both sides' anxious caution, and the cutting winter wind that blows outside. The music hovers between describing external events and internal emotions, and during her trial there is an extraordinary audio-visual moment. Recalling a country walk with her Revolutionary lover Zheliabov, the gentle strings intertwine sensually but are cut short by the judge's voice, whereupon Sofia looks off-screen as if she too had heard it – a premonition of her fate. Obsessing about the relationship she returns to it several times, the music becoming more and more intensely Tchaikovskian until, with a sudden climactic rush, he kisses her and she tears herself away, not only confirming her purity and innocence but even now conforming to the Stalinist injunction not to move outside her main role in life.

But Arnshtam did not always conform to convention. For the last time Shostakovich was writing music to accompany a Revolutionary party, but the camera careers after the dancers much more freely than in other films, and there is no political discussion; just Zheliabov's declaration of love. The music for their walk home is in Shostakovich's 1930s 'triumphant' style, raising questions about how positive a moment this is; it will, after all, lead to both their deaths. The following bedroom scene is a tense nocturne, the camera prowling the room; Soviet films were still puritanical, and this was probably to avoid embarrassing the audience by concentrating on the lovers.[29] The strings throb and the melody is touched in by harp and celeste, as Shostakovich would often do in his late compositions. The strain of her good works and Revolutionary activity tells, and when Sofia feels sick the music rears up against her illness with interjections from the bell, before she dreams of kissing Zheliabov in a celestial white room, their sensual music in the background. Fortunately, she overcomes the illness moving on to the assassination – a series of freeze-frames, skirling music again being suddenly cut off before she catatonically returns to wash her hands like Lady Macbeth, to the erratic heartbeat of the harp. But Arnshtam and Shostakovich have one more trick up their sleeves. The hanging of the Tsaricides brings us back to the beginning of the film with the silly piccolo and side drum march. The drummers stop but the piccolo continues looping the circular melody, to the consternation of his colleagues, until the captain approaches: 'Fool! Stop the music. That's all.' The errant musician hiccups and the film ends, denying us a glorious Zoyaesque coda, and questioning the value of the People's Will.

It is unfortunate for Shostakovich's film reputation that *Sofia Perovskaia* is not better known. Its subject may be a deterrent, bringing expectations of worthy dullness, yet it is very firmly in his late style and bears comparison with other, better-regarded scores. Not only that, but the music explains Perovskaia's personality better than Alexandra Nazarova's monotone performance. Though ostensibly a strong character who breaks with her past, the regular trembling strings speak of her gentler side, taken by the suffering of the people as much as Zheliabov's interest in her. At several points the score is stylistically reminiscent of the Thirteenth Symphony, with its description of Anna Frank waiting for the Nazis, just as Sofia seems to sense her fate.

However outspoken Shostakovich was becoming, the state continued to propose him as 'a loyal son', and Gendelshtein, having returned to non-fiction after *Love and Hate* and *Lermontov*, took this line in the documentary *Dmitri Shostakovich: Sketches Towards a Portrait of the Composer* [Dmitri Shostakovich: Eskizy k portretu kompozitora, 1967].[30] Against that, Alexander Sokurov and

Semion Aranovich's *Viola Sonata* [Dmitri Shostakovich: Altovaia sonata, 1981], made for the seventh-fifth anniversary of his birth, and which portrayed him at odds with the state, was banned. The directors then made the shorter, less contentious *The Composer Shostakovich* [Kompozitor Shostakovich, 1981], completely omitting any discussion of the purges or the events of 1948, which was released, though Sokurov does not acknowledge it.

King Lear [Korol' Lir]

One clue to Shostakovich's commitment to a film project is the quality of the sound editing. Rapid fades and inappropriate cuts imply either that he had other plans for the music or no great interest in it. However, working with certain directors and on certain projects he did take things more seriously and was concerned that his music should be heard properly. One such film was *King Lear*, both Shostakovich and Kozintsev's last completed film, though it was not a conscious 'last statement'; the director considered other projects, in collaboration with Shostakovich. But, in common with many artists' late works, they concentrate on essentials, both in style and content. As with *New Babylon* Shostakovich felt that 'it is not the composer's job to be a musical illustrator. This can be done far more easily by the staff of a music library.'[31]

Continuing his move towards the elemental, Kozintsev set the film in a landscape out of time, 'so very far in the past that it could be some post-neutron-bomb, post-Christian future', and likened it to an abandoned cemetery. Yet 'there is no "desert" in *Lear*, the world of tragedy is densely populated'.[32] To this he added other cultures, particularly Japanese. He saw every production of the 1928 Kabuki Theatre's tour of Russia and knew Akira Kurosawa, who made several Shakespeare films.[33] Later he visited Japan, and was struck not only by Noh theatre and Japanese gardens but also by the museum of Hiroshima. Traces of all of these appear in the film. Kozintsev started to consider *Lear* in about 1967, but among the pre-production problems were difficulties in casting the lead. Yuri Yarvet, the final choice, was an Estonian, who has started his career on a television comedy show and spoke poor Russian, but rather than be dubbed he insisted on improving his accent, though some lines still defeated him so for those he was filmed from behind to make post-synchronisation easier.

Initially, Shostakovich considered turning the commission down. He was ill and could not join the crew, which he felt would hinder the work. 'But my love of Shakespeare, of cinema and my friend Grigori Kozintsev got the upper hand. It was a long and painstaking task. Kozintsev and I had hour-long telephone conversations between Leningrad and Moscow, and I received all the necessary material from him by post. Still, I had to go to Leningrad to round off the work.'³⁴ For Kozintsev, two elements were vital to the film: Pasternak's translation and Shostakovich's music, which 'expressed pity like a force [...] I can hear a ferocious hatred of cruelty, the cult of power and the oppression of justice'.³⁵ In their correspondence about the film music there are repeated requests and promises that the music should be 'sadder'.³⁶

Despite his illness Shostakovich was enthusiastic, though he could not work on it as consistently as he would have liked.³⁷ He eventually wrote seventy cues, though fewer than half of them were used.³⁸ There are over thirty cues but many last only a few seconds, and the score is just half an hour long. Another score using small, flexible cues, it marks an advance in his film music in another way as he moves away from thematic and melodic cues and towards gestural ones. In 1943 Gerald Abrahams had accused Shostakovich of a lack of melodic talent³⁹ (always a questionable charge), but while he could always produce a tune if the work (or his career) needed it, in his later years he turned to pithier music, and *Lear* is one of the scores that, in terms of its language, comes closest to his symphonic works. Again, he carries ideas over from recent works and projects forward to ones that he would write in the future. 'The First Sighting of Lear's Castle' features cautious pizzicato strings with slow, meandering flute and clarinet lines (a texture that reappears in the last movement of the Fifteenth Symphony), while the long crescendi of 'The Storm (Beginning)' is a gesture associated with disaster in the Eighth, Eleventh and Thirteenth Symphonies, the Thirteenth and Fifteenth Quartets, and *Sofia Perovskaia*. It also features a twelve-note row, often seen as a symbol of death in his work. 'Lunch at Goneril's' half echoes Ophelia's music from *Hamlet* and the pawky fanfares of the Second Piano Concerto, though if these are more than fingerprints they could be a comment on paternal inadequacy. It is a theme of both films, and the concerto was dedicated to and premiered by his son Maxim in the midst of Shostakovich's disastrous second marriage. The choral 'People's Lamentation' (one of the few extended pieces) is as motivically tight as the Eighth String Quartet, and the main theme even plays with the intervals that form the *DSCH* monogram, particularly minor thirds – always one of his obsessions, though it opens with a phrase from his next work, the Thirteenth String Quartet.⁴⁰ He conceived in it nine sections to allow the director to pick whichever ones he wanted and reorder them as necessary, though Kozintsev kept the integrity of the piece.⁴¹ At one point Shostakovich feared that even this, the most powerful cue in the film, would be overwhelmed by the images.⁴²

Two important ideas are the fool's music and the three-note 'voice of truth' motif.⁴³ These notes also open 'To Anna Akhmatova', the last of six songs from 1973, dealing with honour, posthumous reputation and the artist's relationship to the state and setting the controversial poet Marina Tsvetaeva, an émigré who returned to the Soviet Union only to commit suicide in 1941.[44] Akhmatova and Shostakovich had a high mutual regard, and she wrote poems dedicated to him and his work, but he neither reciprocated nor set any of her verse, and this is the nearest he came to a direct musical tribute. Shostakovich changed Tsvetaeva's original title 'Oh Weeping Muse', though tears, honesty and thoughts of what is bequeathed to following generations link the film and the poem.

'The Songs of the Fool' are taken from Kozintsev's 1941 staging of *Lear* and, amusingly, are based on 'Jingle Bells', though what inspired this choice is unclear. Two years later, in very different circumstances, he orchestrated 'Eight English and American Folksongs', including 'When Johnny Comes Marching Home' and it may simply have been part of Soviet wartime rapprochement with the West. In January 1970 Glikman suggested a similarity between 'The Songs of the Fool' and 'The Suicide', an Apollinaire setting from the Fourteenth Symphony, and Shostakovich agreed, before throwing back the question as to whether the film or the symphony was the more important work.[45] There are no suicides in *Lear*, and any musical similarity is in tone more than material. On another occasion Shostakovich said: 'Music suits both vaudeville and heroic tragedy. In vaudeville you have to sing the existing couplets and sing them as merrily as possible, whereas in great tragedy the music must, in my opinion, only speak at the moments of highest dramatic tension.'[46]

Both Kozintsev and Shostakovich were fascinated by foolishness, whether the amusing behaviour of the Eccentric clown-fool, Lear and Gloucester's naïvety, or the feigned madness of Edgar (and perhaps Hamlet).[47] As Lear's alter ego, the fool raises questions of morality – and specifically – honesty, mouthing with impunity unpalatable truths that the king dare not admit to himself. The Russian parallel is the *yurodivy*, the 'holy fool', who had just such a relationship with the Tsar. He has the last word in Shostakovich's favourite opera, *Boris Godunov*, and Stroyeva's 1955 film version ends with him sitting in the ruins, awaiting a 'time of trouble', just like the fool in Kozintsev's film (illustration 15, page 106). His music also echoes Mussorgsky's sighing figure ('Flow, flow, bitter tears!'), and the E flat clarinet is reminiscent of the *yurodivy*'s tenor voice. Stroyeva's film ends with these two repeated notes fading away, implying recurring 'times of trouble' – perhaps including the post-Stalin era. Shostakovich's music ends arbitrarily: it is only the end of the film, not of the situation. While Kozintsev worked on the film there was no power struggle in the wake of a ruler's death, but the country was similarly rudderless, gripped by Brezhnev's 'stagnation', following a backlash against Khrushchev's reforms. The former leader was rarely referred to in the press, which criticised earlier 'hare-brained scheming' and there were various repressive measures; 1968 saw both the trial of Ginsburg and Galanskov, for publishing details of the Sinyavsky-Daniel trial, and the invasion of Czechoslovakia.

Lear, despite his physical frailty, retains power over his followers, just as the pock-marked, shrivel-armed Stalin held the country in thrall. Perhaps, like institutionalised patients, some preferred the false security of totalitarianism. The Twelfth and Thirteenth Symphonies, the first dedicated to Lenin and the other condemning the Soviet system's failures, have pointedly consecutive opus numbers. Similarly, he linked his orchestration of *Boris Godunov* with Kozintsev's 1941 staging of *King Lear* by giving them the opus numbers 58 and 58a. Both men are overtaken by events they have initiated but lost control over, and are reminded of their folly by a fool. Kozintsev compresses geography and collapses time to bring together a leader out of control (such as Boris or Stalin) and the barren landscape and rampant corruption of contemporary Brezhnevian stagnation.

After *Hamlet* and *King Lear* Kozintsev considered adding *The Tempest* to make a Shakespearean trilogy, but eventually he wrote *St Petersburg Nights*, a screenplay based on themes from short stories by Gogol. Shostakovich's range of cinema collaborators had been shrinking but he was happy to take this commission, a Gogol project with one of his closest friends. The early 1970s brought the deaths of several of Shostakovich's friends, relatives and collaborators, and, sick himself, this must have made him more aware of his own mortality. Among his cinema colleagues, Mikhail Shapiro, the director of *Katerina Izmailova*, died in 1971, followed in 1972 by Nikolai Rabinovich, a regular conductor of Shostakovich's film soundtracks. But the next year was a particularly bitter one, with the deaths of his elder sister Maria, Lev Atovmian

15. *King Lear*: the *yurodivy*, with the last (musical) word

(who had compiled so many of the suites), and Kozintsev. This was a devastating blow, bringing both the film *St Petersburg Nights* and Shostakovich's cinema career to an end. It closed the loop in two ways: with the director who, with Leonid Trauberg, had been his first cinema collaborator; and with Gogol, the writer who had brought them together. Ailing and with few director friends left, Shostakovich finally withdrew completely from the cinema, completing a dozen or so works for the concert hall before dying on 9 August 1975.

7. Legacy

Shostakovich's cinema career began with great and innovative scores that explored the role of music in the cinema and acted as an incentive to improve both the technical and musical sides of the industry. His early reputation was as an avant-gardist, and *New Babylon* threw down a challenge to cinema musicians, and to other composers, by beginning to develop a new audio-visual grammar – though for technical and political reasons few took it up. *Alone* continued the musico-dramatic innovations but also stretched the technical side of film; the innovations were continued in *The Counterplan*, which further developed the film song after which he went on to help initiate the other strand of Soviet film score writing – the symphonic – with films such as *The Golden Mountains*. As artistic theories settled into Socialist Realism Shostakovich worked on the *Maxim* trilogy, which saw the beginning of an accommodation that was intensified with the *Pravda* editorials, which might make us expect that the cinema would be simply a way to get by financially. After the 1936 denunciations it is clear that he was less interested in cinema as a means of expression than as a source of income, but, even so, he had to hope it would also bring political rewards. Yet there were still scores, such as *Girlfriends*, with a surprising degree of innovation. Hopefully, the results would be favourably looked on, but there was always the danger of adverse political fall-out even in these projects, and such excursions became more difficult. Many of the films Shostakovich worked on suffered political problems, yet his approach could be dismissive – surely a risky attitude, especially as the first peak of his involvement, the late 1930s, was a highpoint of repression as well as being his main source of income. Yet it was not unalloyed misery; some films brought real pleasure and inspiration, though this decreased with the onset of the Cold War, with projects such as *The Fall of Berlin* and *Meeting on the Elbe*.

In the 1950s and 1960s modernism advanced over music, influencing composers who were coming of age during the Thaw. Ironically for a composer whose early reputation was for being at the cutting edge, Shostakovich, eschewing avant-garde techniques, appeared to have been left behind musically. Meanwhile, some were disappointed that he appeared not to take full advantage of the post-Stalin atmosphere to lend his weight to anti-government activities, but he had always tended to be pragmatically private about his resistance, making such public compromises as were necessary to achieve his ends. Writing to Stalin to ask that friends and fellow composers' plights be eased hardly counts as a moral collapse, but even if it were not explicitly spelt out it would have entailed toeing the line in some other way. Musically, he did stay true to traditional forms and conventional ensembles, but it is unlikely that this was one of those compromises. He saw himself as a continuation of the tradition rather than a radical break from it. As a young man he enjoyed using unusual instruments, and when, with dodecaphony a contentious issue in Soviet music, he began to use twelve-note melodies in the early 1960s he defended it by saying that any technique was valid as long as it did not become an end in itself – a counter to possible charges of formalism, though when electronics and pre-recorded tapes became available he stayed away from them.

As with other composers of his generation (Dmitri Kabalevsky, Khachaturian, etc.), Shostakovich's film scores kept stylistic pace with his concert works, whereas some members of the avant-garde tended to approach the work in a very different way. The apparently uncompromisingly severe Galina Ustvolskaya drained off her own personality to produce state-sponsored scores in a wholly acceptable Soviet style, which she could divorce herself from so completely that even to compile a list of them would be a daunting task.[1] Alfred Schnittke used film scores to test and develop ideas for his concert works in a much more extensive way than Shostakovich; film and concert works from quite different periods may rework or even share unaltered material. Nikolai Karetnikov took this a stage further by including parts of his filmically structured and *Nose*-like opera *Till Eulenspiegel* in various official works, including film scores and, by using out-takes from recording sessions and paying performers, compiled a 'samizdat' recording of the work.[2] Shostakovich's film and concert works tend to revolve around each other more closely chronologically but loosely materially. Shared materials often come from the same era, and even when there is no contemporary material in common there is a common style, albeit not always with the same level of intensity. But in one way Schnittke and Shostakovich are similar in their film work: both took structural ideas from cinema for use in their concert music. Just as the films *The Glass Accordion* [Steklannyi garmon, 1968] and *Nevertheless I Believe* [Tak vse ia veriu, 1972–74] inspired Schnittke's polystylism and provided material for his concert music, so Shostakovich, especially at the beginning and end of his career, approached his film and concert pieces as a two-way street.

After 1960, illness and disappointment led Shostakovich to withdraw from the cinema, choosing projects more carefully but often investing more in them. He was musically evolutionary rather than revolutionary, and though in his last years he was not at the outer fringes of the avant-garde the later film scores pick up the exploratory attitude of his earlier work. Not only do the late films show an interest in an evolving audio-visual landscape but especially in the last two, *Hamlet* and *King Lear*, we see flaring up again the uncompromising anger and wit of the younger man, producing a final condemnation of the regime under which he had spent most of his life.

In the years after his death the range of approaches to film scoring diversified. Older composers continued to write symphonic scores while song scores were driven by pop with composers such as Andrei Petrov and Boris Grebenshchikov, extending further into rock with Viktor Tsoi and the group Akvarium. At the same time the electronic experiments of the 1960s and 70s were extended to produce more complex soundtracks where music, speech and sound effects were interwoven. Directors sometimes took a more active role in these, making it harder to separate each contribution, for example Eduard Artemev's work on Tarkovsky's films, Oleg Yanchenko and Elem Klimov with *Come and See* [Idi i smotri, 1985] and the films of Alexander Sokurov. Ironically this is exactly the kind of approach that Shostakovich was developing in his early sound films.

Shostakovich worked on almost forty films by twenty-one directors. These films have several recurring features, but though he is the common element this is not always due to his influence, despite his involvement sometimes extending beyond writing the score. Until recently the West's view of Soviet cinema has largely been auteurist, taking the director as the most important creative force, perhaps because of the international dominance of a few figures. But it has meant that others have been overlooked: few non-specialists could name a Soviet cinematographer or, beyond a couple of stars (Cherkasov or Smoktunovsky, perhaps), any actors. Shostakovich did not work with the two best-known Soviet auteurs, Eisenstein and Tarkovsky; the opportunity did not arise with the first, and the second was younger and wedded to his own collaborators. Nevertheless, with Kozintsev, he supported *Andrei Rublev* [1966] and Tarkovsky hoped the composer could persuade Solzhenitsyn to see it, and when *The Mirror* [Zerkalo, 1974] ran into problems Tarkovsky again turned to him.[3]

Hence Shostakovich's cinema career was built with figures who, for a variety of reasons, are less prominent. Some were or became politically contentious (Chiaureli, Ermler), and some were victims of a combination of factors (Kozintsev and Trauberg), and, when he did work with well-known names, they were sometimes producing less than their best work (Dovzhenko, Alexandrov).

But in the absence of a single director, and with a limited role for Shostakovich, these common themes and elements show that there are other influences on the films. On a surface level there are recurrent scenes, such as parties or music used to mask political activity; and elements such as the political mentor showing the ingénu hero the way, or visual motifs such as Yutkevich's despised 'Lenin on the telephone' scenes. Musically there are common textures, such as the extensive use of folk and Revolutionary songs, with particular tunes proving especially popular. But, beyond that, there are broader themes: post-Stalin cinema's fascination with father figures is a major part of Kozintsev and Shostakovich's *Hamlet* and *King Lear* but it also crops up in many other films, from *Ballad of a Soldier* [Ballada o soldate, 1959], directed by Grigori Chukhrai, to his son Pavel's *The Thief* [Vor, 1997]. These are not themes or elements generated solely by Shostakovich or even by the directors or writers. In a way, these elements show the auteur to be the state itself, or perhaps, in the case of Stalinist cinema, its leader. Given his contributions to scripts, it is easy to argue that he was an unacknowledged writer – and the most important.

Past studies of Shostakovich have relegated his film work to passing mentions and brief footnotes; many times there has been no discussion of the plots, themes or – bizarrely in books about a composer – the music. A common idea is that the cinema was a cosy corner into which he could withdraw, safe from the political buffeting that his concert works were exposed to. But this position is hard to support: many of his concert works suffered bans, while cinema – 'the most important art' – was correspondingly closely watched. While it certainly provided him with a much-needed income it was far from a politically anodyne atmosphere, and his apparently minor role in it did not necessarily mean it would be overlooked, even when it was not specifically mentioned. While Alexandrov and Dunaevsky were making their Stalinist musical comedy *Volga Volga*, ongoing press reports listed different crew members as people were exiled or arrested;[4] there was political intervention on all the films that Shostakovich worked on, and many encountered problems. Cinema workers walked a tightrope between being feted and being fated. Shostakovich knew this, but had no choice but to continue.

Notes

Introduction

1 The precise number depends on how two-part films are counted. For example, the two halves of *The Young Guard* [Molodaia gvardiia, 1948] were released separately but are generally counted as a single film. *The Fall of Berlin* [Padenie Berlina, 1950] was released as a single film in the Soviet Union but as two in some other countries.
2 G.M. Boltianskii (ed.), *Lenin i kino*, Moscow/Leningrad, 1925, pp.16–19. R. Taylor (co-ed. and trans.) and I. Christie (co-ed.) *The Film Factory: Russian and Soviet Cinema in Documents*, London, 1988, pp.56–57 (henceforth *FF*). By the time Commissar for Enlightenment Anatoli Lunacharsky's report of this conversation was published, the leader was dead and unable to confirm it. Lenin liked newsreels: Lunacharsky scripted and starred in fiction films.
3 S.M. Volkov *Testimony: The Memoirs of Dmitri Shostakovich as related to and edited by Solomon Volkov*, London, 1981.
4 The interpolations were revealed in L. Fay, 'Shostakovich versus Volkov: Whose Testimony?' *Russian Review*, vol. 39, no. 4 (1980), pp.484–493. For a rebuttal of the case against *Testimony*, see A.B. Ho and D. Feofanov, *Shostakovich Reconsidered*, London, 1998. A rebuttal of the rebuttal then appeared: M.H. Brown, *A Shostakovich Casebook*, Indiana, 2004.
5 Early in Dziga Vertov's *The Man with a Movie Camera* [Chelovek s kinoapparatom, 1929] we see a medium-sized cinema orchestra preparing to accompany... *The Man with a Movie Camera*.
6 Shostakovich, 'Avtobiografiia', *Sovetskaia muzyka*, no. 9, 1966, p.25. L.G. Grigoriev [Ginzburg] and Ya.M. Platek (trans. A. and N. Roxburgh), *Dmitry Shostakovich: About His Life and His Times*, Moscow, 1981, p.13. Henceforth *G&P*. This book was part of the Soviet response to *Testimony*. Other sources imply Shostakovich began the work not in 1923 but in autumn 1924. L. Fay, *Shostakovich: A Life*, Oxford, 2000, p.23.
7 His name appears on a Svetlaia lenta poster for Tuesday 23 December 1924. The film he accompanied, *A Temporary Husband* [Vremennyi muzh], is not listed in

A.V. Macheret (ed.), *Sovetskie khudozhestvennye fil'my: annotirovannyi katalog*, tom 1, Moscow, 1961. It was probably *Temporary Marriage* [USA, 1923].
8   V.I. Seroff. *Dmitri Shostakovich: The Life and Background of a Soviet Composer*, New York, 1943, p.124.
9   Volkov, pp.6–7.
10 Seroff, pp.123–124.
11 J. Leyda, *Kino: A History of Russian and Soviet Film*, London, 1983, p.190.
12 Shostakovich, 'Zhiznepisanie Dmitria Dmitrievicha Shostakovicha', *G&P*, p.10.
13 Shostakovich, 'Avtobiografiia'.
14 Oksana Dvornichenko, *Shostakovich*. (DVD-ROM), Chandos CHAN 55001, 2000.
15 N.V. Lukyanova (Yu. Shirokov trans.), *Shostakovich*, Neptune City, 1984, p.33.
16 D.J. Youngblood, *Soviet Cinema in the Silent Era, 1918–1935*. Ann Arbor, MI, 1985, p.61. Some reports did seep out into the Western press.
17 B.S.Ol'khovyi (ed.) *Puti kino: Vsesoiuznoe partiinoe soveshchanie po kinematografii*, Moscow, 1929, pp.429–444 [translated as 'Party Cinema Conference Resolution: The Results of Cinema Construction in the USSR and the Tasks of Soviet Cinema']; *FF*, pp.208–215.
18 S.M. Eisenstein, G.V. Alexandrov and V.I. Pudovkin, 'Statement on Sound', *S.M. Eisenstein: Selected Works*, vol. 1, *Writings 1922–1934* (R. Taylor ed. and trans.), London, pp.113–114.
19 *S.M. Eisenstein: Selected Works*, vol. 2, *Towards a Theory of Montage* (M. Glenny co-ed. and trans., R. Taylor co-ed.), London, 1991, pp.250–251.
20 In common with other classic silent films, *Potemkin* was later re-released with synchronised music, including a re-edited version of Meisel (*c.* 1930), a new score by Nikolai Kriukov (1950s) and selections from Shostakovich (1967), though he was little involved in this.
21 Y. Tsivian, 'Dziga Vertov's Frozen Music: Cue Sheets and a Music Scenario for *The Man with a Movie Camera*', *Griffithiana*, no.54 (October 1995), pp.93–121. The Alloy Orchestra's realisation of Vertov's instructions can be heard on the DVD and video of the film released by the BFI.
22 A facsimile was published in Moscow in 1990. Annotated translation in *FF*, pp.58–64. For a different, unannotated version, see M. Pytel and G. Dadomo, *Eccentrism*, London, 1992.
23 Director Lev Kuleshov claimed that cinema was more closely related to circus than theatre. L.V. Kuleshov, 'Circus-Cinema-Theatre', *Selected Works: Fifty Years in Film*, Moscow, 1987, pp.62–64.
24 Multimedia experiments were popular in the 1920s, Eisenstein initially considered having the prow of a ship burst through the screen at the end of *The Battleship Potemkin*.

Chapter 1

1   The title of an article by Viktor Shklovsky; 'Beregites' muzyki', *Sovetskii ekran*, 1 January 1929, p.6. *FF*, pp.251–252.
2   For an overview of melodies that have been suggested as its inspiration (none of which bears much resemblance to it), see D.C. Hulme, 'Shostakovich and Fried Chicken', *DSCH*, no. 7 (May–June 1988), pp.6–7.

3   Translations use permutations of *Hypothetically, Allegedly, Conditionally* or *Declared*, and *Killed, Dead* or *Murdered*.
4   B.S. Ol'khovyi, *FF*, p.212.
5   Trauberg claimed that it was a response to Konstantin Mardzhanov's *The Communard's Pipe* [Trubka kommunara, 1929] but that only opened in Tiflis on 14 February 1929. Perhaps it was a response to the news that Kozintsev's friend was working on the film.
6   The contract was for a fourteen-piece orchestra, but the score requires around thirty players.
7   T. van Houten, *Leonid Trauberg and his Films: Always the Unexpected*, Hertogenbosch, the Netherlands, 1989, p.41.
8   Kozintsev claimed that he also accompanied their film *The Devil's Wheel* [Chertovo koleso, 1926] but this only opened after he had left the pit. Perhaps he did it as a favour in pre-release screenings.
9   G.M. Kozintsev, *Glubokii ekran*, Moscow, 1971, p.101.
10 G.M. Kozintsev, *King Lear: The Space of Tragedy*, London, 1977, p.243.
11 For translations of some of the cinema conference speeches see *FF*, pp.241–245, and 250–251. NEP = New Economic Policy, introduced in 1921 and marking a return to mixed economy.
12 He complained that popular films were projected at a faster speed, allowing a profitable second showing but ruining the music.
13 *Sovietskii ekran*, no. 11, 1929, p.3. This is one of the most important texts on Shostakovich's film work and his general aesthetic at the time, yet it has rarely been reproduced in full. The first complete English translation appeared in M. Pytel, *New Babylon*, London, 1999, pp.24–26.
14 Ibid.
15 The only complete recording to date (Capriccio 10 341-2, Berlin RSO/James Judd) is in eight parts, but the directors wrote of seven reels. Kozintsev and Trauberg, 'Novyi Vavilon', *Sovetskii ekran*, no. 32, December 1928, pp.8–9. Reproduced and translated in Pytel, pp.81–82.
16 D. Robinson, 'When Film Making was All about Circus and Scandal'. *Times* (London), 20 January 1983, p.8; van Houten, *Always the Unexpected*, p.151.
17 F. Dostoevsky (trans. D Magarshak), *The Devils*, London, 1971, pp.326–327.
18 B.S.Ol'khovyi, *FF*, pp.208–215.
19 Estimates respectively from *Iz istorii Lenfil'ma* vol. 1, Leningrad, 1968, p.256, and Pytel, p.28.
20 Pytel, p.60.
21 Volkov, p.114. The infamous Pravda editorial on *Lady Macbeth* concludes that things 'may end badly'. 'Sumbur vmesto muzyki: ob opere Ledi Makbet Mtsenskogo uezda', *Pravda*, 28 January 1936, p.3. [Muddle Instead of Music: About the Opera *Lady Macbeth of the Mtsensk District*]. Reproduced and translated in *DSCH*, no. 12 (April/May 1989), pp.3–7.
22 One of Shostakovich's favourite sayings was that his musical tastes went 'from Bach to Offenbach'.
23 Including his *Scherzo*, opus 7 (1924), which at that time he called his *Officer's Scherzo*. It has no military overtones in the film.
24 D. Shostakovich, 'Kak rozhdaetsia muzyka', *Literaturnaia gazeta*, 21 December 1965.
25 Shostakovich's ballets and theatre music are full of recyclings and subtle (and not so subtle) variations on previous pieces.

26 V.B. Shklovskii, 'Kinoiazyk *Novogo Vavilona' Podenshchina*; Leningrad, 1930, pp.147–157. [The Film Language of *New Babylon*]; *FF*, pp.311–313.
27 P. Sobolevskii, *Iz zhizni kinoaktera*, Moscow, 1967, pp.85–116.
28 James Judd's recording (Capriccio 10341/42) uses the Sikorski edition. Conductor Mark FitzGerald discusses the differences between the two scores in J. Riley, '*New Babylon* in Rotterdam', *DSCH*, no. 16 January 2002, pp.50–51.
29 A phrase used by Pavel Petrov-Bytov in explicitly and repeatedly criticising *New Babylon*. 'U nas net sovetskoi kinematografii', *Zhizn' iskusstva*, 21 April 1929, p.8 [We Have No Soviet Cinema]; *FF*, pp.259–262.
30 Character and actress share a name – a feature of several films of the time.
31 On whether the split between the 'avant-garde' and the 'proletarians' was as pronounced as has been suggested in the past, see N. Edmunds, 'The Ambiguous Origins of Socialist Realism and Musical Life in the Soviet Union', in G. Chew et al. (eds), *Socialist Realism and Music: Anti-Modernisms and Avant-Gardes*, Prague, Bärenreiter-Verlag, forthcoming.
32 L. Arnshtam, 'Zlatye gory', *Sovetskii ekran*, no. 23, 1971, p.18.
33 van Houten, p.144.
34 B. Shumiatskii, *Kinematografiia millionov*, Moscow, 1935, p.117.
35 'At that time the way to a truly artistic combination of sound and image was still being sought.' D. Shostakovich, 'Kino kak shkola kompozitora', in D. Eremin (ed.), *30 let sovetskoi kinematografii: sbornik statei*, Moscow, 1950, p.354. Extracts in *G&P*, pp.133–135.
36 According to Tatiana Egorova, 'the banality of the poster/slogan idea underlying [*The Concrete Sets*] resulted in an inexpressive, neutral background of sometimes openly illustrative "film music", which [Shostakovich] chose subsequently to forget'; *Soviet Film Music*, Amsterdam, 1997, p.289. I have discovered no other references to the completion of this film.
37 'Deklaratsiia obiazannostei kompozitora', *Rabochii i teatr*, no. 31 (20 November 1931), p.6. Extracts in Lukyanova, *Shostakovich*, p.71.
38 Eremin, p.354.
39 Eremin, p.355.
40 The similarity to Emile Waldteufel's waltz *Violettes* is coincidental.
41 He reused this in the operetta *Cheremushki*, which is a veritable repository of such borrowings and the return to his youthful liking for popular song.
42 'The Soviet Cinema', *British Russian Gazette and Trade Outlook*, September 1933, pp.311–314.
43 Interview with Oksana Dvornichenko. Chandos DVD-ROM.
44 S. Khentova, *Shostakovich*. Cited in sleevenotes of RD CD 11 064.
45 Y. Barna, *Eisenstein*, London, 1973, p.177. Leyda wrote the foreword but does not discuss the music. Shostakovich is not mentioned in Harry Geduld and Ronald Gottesman, *The Making and Unmaking of Qué viva México*, Bloomington, 1970.
46 In an aural equivalent of *The Man with a Movie Camera*, it starts with shots of Popov's soundtrack being recorded.
47 M. Turovskaya, 'The 1930s and 1940s: Cinema in Context', R. Taylor and D. Spring (eds), *Stalinism and Soviet Cinema*, London, 1993, p.44.
48 Other translations include *Shame, Coming Your Way, The Passer-by, Morning Light* and *Turbine 50,000*. The working title was *Greeting the Future*.
49 P. Kenez, *Cinema and Soviet Society from the Revolution to the Death of Stalin*, London, 2001, p.151.

50 Shumiatskii praised the characterisation, but Ilia Ehrenburg said that 'Mannequins are mannequins'; *FF*, pp.331, 395.
51 Cited in G. Hosking, *A History of the Soviet Union, 1917–1991*, London, 1992, p.174.
52 Letter to Vissarion Shebalin (October 1931).
53 S. Khentova, *V mire Shostakovicha*, Moscow, 1996, pp.125–126, 141. See also S. Khentova (trans. V. Dvortsov), 'The Khentova Interviews: Abram Abramovich Ashkenazy', *DSCH*, 20, pp.7–11, which relates what happened when Alexander Cherniavsky (real name Tsymbal) claimed to have written the melody.
54 In 1933, of 32,000 projectors only about 200 were equipped for sound; Youngblood, p.222.
55 Eremin, p.355.
56 Ibid.
57 A completely different opening scene more reminiscent of *Alone* is described in Egorova, pp.31–32.
58 HTS (Harry T. Smith), 'Soviet Machine Romance', *New York Times*, 11 March 1933.
59 R. Bond, 'Counter Plan' [sic], *Close Up*, 10, no. 2, June 1933, pp.197–198.
60 K. London, *Film Music: A Summary of the Characteristic Features of its History, Aesthetics, Technique; and Possible Developments*, London, 1936, pp.178, 244–245. With music by Shebalin, S. Germanov and Nikolai Kriukov, *Men and Jobs* uses similar effects.
61 Shostakovich reused it in the cantata *The Poem of the Motherland* (1947), the films *Michurin* [1948] and *The Song of the Rivers* [1954], and the operetta *Moscow Cheremushki* [1959, filmed in 1962 with the name of the city dropped from the title].

Chapter 2

1 Some sources list *Genu in Pilae* (1934). Supposedly destroyed by order of Stalin, with a score recreated from orchestral parts, its existence was invented as a practical joke. The title is Latin for *A Kick in the Balls*.
2 See E.I. Shub, *Krupnym planom*, Moscow, 1958, pp.153–158. S.I. Yutkevich, *Kino – eto pravda 24 kadra v sekundu*. Moscow, 1974, pp.68–69; and L. and J. Schnitzler, *Youtkévitch ou la permanence de l'avant-garde*, Paris, 1976, pp.173–175. Shub includes two photographs taken on location, and there are some stills in Yutkevich. None discusses Shostakovich's music.
3 Balda is a common Russian name for an idiot, and various alternative translations reflect this.
4 There have been at least two other film versions: one from 1939 (director Pantaleimon Sazonov, music Iosif Kovner), and one from 1956 (director Anatoli Karanovich, music Nikolai Peiko). Kozintsev and Yutkevich staged a puppet version in Kiev in 1919, and Shostakovich probably discussed it with them.
5 Volkov, p.13. Kustodiev's portrait of Shostakovich aged thirteen was the composer's favourite. His Leskov illustrations were used in the first edition of the score of Shostakovich's *Lady Macbeth of Mtsensk*.
6 S. Ginzburg, *Risovannyi i kukol'nyi fil'm*, Moscow, 1957, p.146.
7 The surviving fragment, 'Scene at the Bazaar', was shown at the 1967 Moscow Film Festival and can be seen on the DVD-ROM Shostakovich (Chandos, CHAN 55001).

8   In 1980 Sofia Khentova compiled a seventy-five minute opera, supplementing the fragments with other Shostakovich works.
9   Tsekhanovsky regarded Shostakovich highly, describing him in his diary as 'a real artist. A real master', and feeling that he would have to raise his game to match the composer.
10 Shostakovich, 'Schast'e poznania', *Sovetskoe iskusstvo*, 5 November 1934, p.5.
11 He revived the part again in Sergei Gerasimov's short *Meeting with Maxim* [Vstrecha s Maksimom, 1941].
12 *Russian River*, his 1944 NKVD Song and Dance Ensemble 'spectacle', includes a movement entitled *Football*. The NKVD (People's Commissariat for Internal Affairs) was a forerunner of the KGB (Committee for State Security).
13 'Lektsii G.M Kozintseva chitannye vo VGIKe v 1937/38 uchebnom godu', *Iz istorii Lenfil' ma*, vol. 4, Leningrad, p.112.
14 The scene is preceded by prisoners sending a message by tapping on the walls, an effect Shostakovich reproduced when setting Apollinaire's 'In the Santé Prison' in his Fourteenth Symphony (1969).
15 Also known as Symphony in A, it included the 'Marseillaise', the 'Internationale', 'Varshavyanka' and 'the funeral march', which may well have been 'You Fell as a Victim'. V. Tolstoy, I. Bibikova and C. Cooke (eds) *Street Art of the Revolution: Festivals and Celebrations in Russia, 1918–1933*. London, 1990, pp.146–147.
16 Iuli Raizman's *The Communist* [Kommunist, 1958] faced just that question. J. Woll, *Soviet Cinema and the Thaw*, London, 2000, p.84.
17 G. Kozintsev and L. Trauberg, 'The Youth of Maxim', *Izvestiia*, 14 December 1934; *FF*, pp.338.
18 Neya Zorkaya, *The Illustrated History of the Soviet Cinema*, New York, 1989, p.195.
19 'Sumbur vmesto muzyki'.
20 'Baletnaia fal'sh'', *Pravda*, 6 February 1936, p.3.
21 'Sumbur vmesto muzyki'.
22 It is dedicated to Romain Rolland, 'friend of the Soviet Union'. His seventieth birthday in January 1936 had been impressively marked by *Pravda*, using the same phrase. In April a request that Shostakovich write music for a staging of his *Liluli* came to nothing.
23 Yutkevich oversaw a later restoration of the film, adding the second movement of the First String Quartet (1938) to the credit sequence.
24 Anastasia Verbitskaia's popular novel *The Keys to Happiness* (1909–1913) concerns a headstrong young woman.
25 Shostakovich reused the song in his Eighth String Quartet. See pp.88.
26 It may have been simple carelessness that led to both this film and *The Youth of Maxim* sharing an opus number (41), or it may be a reflection of how highly he regarded them. Various ways have been devised to differentiate them. Three short, unpublished fragments from *The Girlfriends* have been recorded.
27 *Kinematograph Weekly*, 21 May 1936, p.15.
28 Cited in R. Prendergast, *Film Music: a Neglected Art*, New York and London, 1992, p.47.
29 Shostakovich, *Collected Works*, vol. 41, Moscow, 1987, Introduction.
30 Isaac Babel, *Collected Stories* (intro. by Lionel Trilling), London, 1961, pp.11–12.
31 Elizabeth Wilson, *Shostakovich: A Life Remembered*, London, 1994, pp.123–125.
32 Both Lev Atovmian and Konstantin Fortunatov made chamber arrangements.

33 Hence the alternative titles *Dal'nii vostok* (*The Far East*) and *Interventsiia na dal'nem vostoke* (*Intervention in the Far East*). Having been released as *The Defense of Volotchayevsk* in America in 1938 it was cut from 112 to 90 minutes and reopened on 26 August 1942 as *The Battle for Siberia*.
34 Shostakovich, 'Moi blizhaishchie raboty', *Rabochii i teatr*, no. 11 (November 1937), p.24. Partly translated in *G&P*, pp.69–70.
35 Apart from those in films and stage plays, his songs included four of a planned (but uncompleted) set of twelve Pushkin settings, which he referred to later in the conference speech, and six Japanese songs. I. Ioffe, *Muzyka sovetskogo kino*, Moscow, 1938; *G&P*, p.71.
36 Many composers reused material in this way. For the 1968 re-release of *The Mother* [*Mat*', 1926] Khrennikov used excerpts from his opera.
37 Tell's failure in the opera may parallel the Japanese failure in the film.
38 Shostakovich, 'Moi blizhaishichie raboty', *Rabochii i teatr*, no. 11, 1937, p.24.
39 When first recorded the song was attributed to Alexander Alexandrov and S. Alymov, but this was later changed to I. Aturov and Piotr Parfenov. The correct attribution remains mysterious.
40 *Pravda*, 12 September 1967.
41 The film was screened at the Academy Cinema in London on 26 November 1939 (*Society for Cultural Relations Annual Report*, 1940). Two 1938 recordings have appeared on CD, with one described as 'copied from optical soundtrack' and perhaps taken from the film.
42 Shostakovich, 'Moi blizhaishchie raboty'.
43 Piotrovsky was the author of the play *Rule Britannia* (1931) and the much-criticised ballet *The Limpid Stream* (1935), both with music by Shostakovich. He was purged.
44 Scriptwriters Mikhail Bleiman, Mikhail Bolshintsev and Ermler wrote an article about the delays. 'Rabota nad stsenariem', *Iskusstvo kino*, no. 5 (May 1938), pp.30–31.
45 A. Latyshev, 'Stalin i kino', in Iu. Senokosov (ed.), *Surovaia drama naroda*, Moscow, 1989, p.494.
46 The script had been ordered in 1935, but it was not approved until 1937. G. Ermolaev, 'Chto tormozit razvitie sovetskogo kino?', *Pravda*, 9 January 1938, p.4 ['What is Holding up the Development of Soviet Cinema?']; *FF*, p.386.
47 The source of his name has caused confusion. Some claim he is named after the film's hero, and some Shostakovich's uncle Maxim Kostrychkin, an Old Bolshevik who was purged in 1937. Maxim has denied the latter.
48 See Alexander Sesonske, 'Re-editing History: *Lenin in October* Then and Now', *Sight and Sound*, vol. 53. no. 1, pp.56–58.
49 Ermolaev; *FF*, p.386.
50 Pogodin's *Aristocrats* (1934–1935) is similarly structured. White Sea Canal slave workers are portrayed as anti-social individualists who become positive members of society through work and the guidance of the beneficent guards. It has been described as being 'as rich in comedy as a Chaplin film'. André van Gyseghem, *Theatre in Soviet Russia*, London, 1943, p.202.
51 In 1957 Yutkevich wrote to Shtraukh decrying such clichés, citing 'Lenin talks on the telephone'. Stills of such offending scenes appear in innumerable books and journal articles.
52 'The Khentova Interviews: Abraham Abramovich Ashkenazy', *DSCH*, 20, pp.7–11.

53 G&P, p.165.
54 *Izbrannie stsenarii sovetskogo kino*, tom 2, Moscow, 1949. Among others, this also includes the scripts of the Shostakovich-scored *Volochaev Days* and *The Great Citizen*. Stills with Stalin appear in N. Pogodin, 'Chelovek s ruzh'em', *Iskusstvo kino*, no. 12 (December 1939), pp.14–15.
55 L. and J. Schnitzer and M. Martin (ed. and trans. D. Robinson), *Cinema in Revolution: The Heroic Age of the Soviet Film*, London, 1973, p.92.
56 Vertov's short film *Octoberisation* [1921] shows just such a ceremony, culminating in everyone singing the 'Internationale'.
57 Zorkaya, p.145. The trilogy ends with Maxim unequivocally turning to the audience: 'Farewell, comrades!'
58 For before and after stills, see R. Taylor and D. Spring (eds), *Stalinism and Soviet Cinema*, London, 1993, p.162. Maxim's meeting with Stalin was also cut, though stills appear in the contemporary script; Kozintsev and Trauberg, *Trilogiia o Maksima*, Moscow, 1939.
59 V.A. Bakun and I.V. Sepman (eds), *Fridrikh Ermler: Dokumenty, stat'i, vospominaniia*, Leningrad, 1974, pp.197–198. As the filmography includes only completed work, this is not included.
60 'Novye raboty D Shostakovicha', *Leningradskaia pravda*, 28 August 1939.
61 N. Kovarskii, *Fridrikh Ermler*, Moscow, 1941. Much of pages 34 to 89 (out of 96) deals with the film.
62 N.M. Lary, *Dostoevsky and Soviet Film: Visions of Demonic Realism*, Ithaca, NY, 1986, pp.65–80. The chapter title underlines the conflict between self-expression and political conformity: 'Ermler's Pure Art of the Party Line'.

Chapter 3

1 Shostakovich, 'Muzyka v kino. Zametki kompozitora', *Literaturnaia gazeta*, 10 April 1939, p.5. *G&P*, pp.78–79.
2 Satie wrote several barless works from the 1880s onwards.
3 S.S. Prokofiev, 'S.S. Prokof'ev pishet muzyku k fil'mu', *Muzykal'naia zhizn'*, no. 16, August 1983, pp.18–19.
4 Volkov claims that the film was lost, but this must be a confusion with *The Tale of the Priest*.
5 In, among other places, 'Muzyka v kino', where he discusses the idea at length.
6 Leonid claimed that Ilia (1903–1948) was murdered when he got back together with his ex-wife, who was by then married to 'a very high [German] official' named Reichmann, though he admitted to having no proof. Van Houten, p.131.
7 Melik-Pashaev premiered the suite from *The Golden Mountains* in autumn 1931.
8 There are two- or four-hand piano transcriptions dating from 1945, 1960 and 1967.
9 *Kontsert masterov iskusstv* (*Concert of Artistic Masters*, 1952), by Gerbert Rappaport (director of *Cheremushki*) climaxes with part of the recent *The Song of the Forests*, and *Kontsert artistov Leningradskoi estrady i teatrov* (*Concert of Leningrad Light Entertainment and Theatre Artists*, 1956) includes an unidentified waltz. A.V. Macharet, *Sovetskie khudozhestvennye fil'my: annotirovannyi katalog*, tom 2, Moscow, 1961; entries 2008 and 2289.
10 For more on this, and specifically Shostakovich's *Declared Dead*, see G.McBurney 'Declared Dead but Only Provisionally: Shostakovich, Soviet Music-hall and

Uslovno Ubityi' in N.Edmunds, *Soviet Music and Society Under Lenin and Stalin: the Baton and Sickle*. London, 2004.
11 *Valeri Chkalov* was shown as *Wings of Victory* at the Stanley Theatre on 14 November 1941. *Concert Waltz* was made in 1940 and released in the USSR on 24 March 1941. Press release in the BFI National Library.
12 It also appears under the credit sequence of the film *David Oistrakh: Artist of the People?* [France, 1994].
13 A friend claimed that Shostakovich thought the only true cinema genius was Chaplin. I. Glikman (trans. A. Phillips), *The Story of a Friendship: The Letters of Dmitry Shostakovich to Isaak Glikman*, London, 2001, p.299. When Peter Pears and Benjamin Britten visited Shostakovich he treated them to a screening of *The Gold Rush*.
14 A ten-minute six-movement suite has been compiled and recorded by Gennadi Rozhdestvensky.

Chapter 4

1 Sources disagree on the month but the correct one is given in the published script: *Izbrannye stsenarii sovetkogo kino*, tom 5, Moscow, 1950.
2 Illustrated in M. Cullerne Bown, *Art Under Stalin*, Oxford, 1991, p.143.
3 *Pravda*, 26 January 1942, p.2. Translated in J. von Geldern and R. Stites (eds), *Mass Culture in Soviet Russia: Tales, Poems, Songs, Movies, Plays and Folklore, 1917–1953*, Bloomington, pp.341–344.
4 The parade features caricature puppets, such as appear in Tolstoy, Bibikova and Cooke.
5 Arnshtam reports that while writing the Eighth Symphony Shostakovich made a point of watching newsreels.
6 In compiling the suites Atovmian frequently used the film's end music as the opening.
7 Galina Vodyanitskaya, who plays Zoya, describing 'My First Role in Pictures' in *Cinema Chronicle*, no. 12, December 1944, pp.6–12.
8 D. Eremin, 'Zoia', *Izvestiia*, 23 September 1944.
9 O. Leonidov, 'Zoia', *Moskovskii bol'shevik*, 24 September 1944.
10 Iu. Kalashnikov et al. *Ocherki istorii sovetkogo kino*, tom 2, Moscow, 1959, p.656.
11 Eremin, *30 Let*, p.356.
12 It is one of his most frequently rearranged pieces, including an orchestration by Stokowski (1935).
13 *Izbrannye stsenarii sovetkogo kino*, tom 5, p.366.
14 *Izbrannye stsenarii sovetkogo kino*, tom 5, p.370.
15 20 June 1942. A newsreel sequence of Shostakovich 'composing' it at the piano was endlessly reused.
16 This brief broadcast, in which he cryptically says that '…our art is in great danger. Let us defend our music', appears as an appendix to Vladimir Ashkenazy's recording of the symphony (Decca 448 814–2).
17 From a CBS press release. Cited in S.C. Smith, *A Heart at Fire's Center*, Berkeley, 1991, p.109. In 1974 Herrmann recorded parts of Shostakovich's score to Kozintsev's *Hamlet*. Sergio Leone's unmade film on the siege of Leningrad was to begin with a close-up of Shostakovich's hands playing the symphony.

18 For a history of the song and its various incarnations, see J. Riley, 'From the Factory to the Flat: Thirty Years of *The Song of the Counterplan*', in N. Edmunds, *Soviet Music Under Lenin and Stalin: The Baton and Sickle*, London, 2004.
19 *Film Chronicle*, nos 1–2 (January–February 1944), p.11; USSR Society for Cultural Relations with Foreign Countries.
20 A full list appears in P. Babitsky and J. Rimberg, *The Soviet Film Industry*, New York, 1955, p.48.
21 *VOKS Cinema Chronicle*, no. 6 (June 1945), pp.27–28.
22 Under 'SocRealizm', (Polish Socialist Realism), Lutosławski's First Symphony was condemned in 1947 as a turning away from populist, folk-music-based pieces.
23 For examples of the criticisms, see Fay, *A Life*, pp.147–148.
24 In the column 'Today and Tomorrow', in *Literature and Art*, 8 July 1944.
25 *Soviet Art*, 21 September 1945.
26 Though, of course, not by Eisenstein, it appears in *S.M. Eisenstein: Selected Works*, vol. 3: *Writings 1934–47*, R. Taylor, (ed.), trans. W. Powell, London, 1996, pp.295–298.
27 The first parts of both Lukov's and Eisenstein's films had won Stalin Prizes. After reshoots and re-editing *Admiral Nakhimov* was released in late 1947. *Simple People* emerged in 1956. Lukov's and Eisenstein's films finally appeared in 1958.
28 Van Houten, p.103.
29 Van Houten, p.166.
30 *Soviet Art*, 16 August 1947.
31 Ibid.
32 Van Houten, pp.155–156. For an example from the height of the campaign, see V. Shcherbina, 'O gruppe estetstvuiushchikh kosmopolitov v kino'. *Iskusstvo kino*, no. 1 (January 1949), pp.14–15.
33 Van Houten, pp.146–147, 153–158, 167–168.
34 Glikman, pp.40, 250.
35 For a list of thematic allusions in the symphony, see D. Fanning, *The Breath of the Symphonist: Shostakovich's Tenth*, London, 1988, pp.79–80.
36 For the full text, see p.vii.
37 Musical biopics may have helped kick start the filmed operas and ballets that became popular in the 1950s and 60s.
38 A. Dovzhenko, notebook, 18 November 1954; M. Carynnyk (ed.), *Alexander Dovzhenko: Poet as Filmmaker*, Cambridge, MA, 1973, p.254.
39 According to the composer's son Maxim: 'You know, Shostakovich never wrote *bad* music. Not even in his theatre and film scores which people sometimes say are bad. That's just not true.' J. Riley and H. van de Groep, 'Maxim on Shostakovich' *DSCH*, no. 16 (January 2002), pp.47–48.
40 'Poema o rodine: kantata Shostakovicha', *Vecherniaia moskva*, 14 November 1947, p.3.
41 See Alexander Werth, *Musical Uproar in Moscow*, London, 1949 – a vivid first-hand account of the conference, with large parts of the proceedings transcribed.
42 Editorial, 'Sovetskim fil'mam – polnotsennuiu muzyku', *Iskusstvo kino*, no. 2 (February 1948), pp.1–2. Many composers are criticised in this article, the first paragraph citing 'Shostakovich, Prokofiev, Khachaturian, Shebalin, Popov, Myaskovsky and others'. The composers appear in the same order as in the Central Committee resolution and the report in *Pravda*, 11 February 1948.
43 Ibid.

44 V. Razhnikov, *Kirill Kondrashin rasskazyvaet o muzyke i zhizni*, Moscow, 1989, p.201.
45 Glikman, p.34.
46 As leader of the Russian Association of Proletarian Writers, Fadeyev signed a letter supporting *New Babylon*. From 1946–1954 he headed the Union of Soviet Writers, but his last novel was judged unacceptable. Haunted by past complicity, he sank into alcoholism and in 1956 shot himself.
47 Eremin, *30 Let*, pp.356–357.
48 19 July 1960; Glikman, pp.90–91. For more on this quote, see pp.88.
49 For instance 'Results of My Sixty Years' Work and Prospects for the Future', in *Transactions of the I.V. Michurin Plant-Breeding Station*, vol. 2, 1934. Reprinted in I.V. Michurin, *Selected Works* (in English), Moscow, 1949.
50 Unlike many places that have reverted to pre-Soviet names, Kozlov is still Michurinsk.
51 Including Viacheslav Lebedev's children's story *Michurin's Dream* (1940) and Semion Kirsanov's poem *Work in the Garden* (1935), with its line: 'Essentially, I'm a Michurinist'.
52 Lysenko's report to the Lenin Academy of Agricultural Sciences (31 July to 7 August 1948). He yokes together the monk Gregor Mendel and the American zoologist Thomas Hunt Morgan.
53 P.N. Yakovlev, 'Introduction', *Ivan Michurin: Works* (in English), p.xix.
54 T. Dobzhansky, 'Russian Genetics', in R.C. Christman (ed.), *Soviet Science*, Washington, 1952, p.1.
55 Autobiography; Carynnyk, p.21.
56 Notebook, 5 April 1948; Carynnyk, p.158.
57 For a fuller analysis of the Byzantine politics behind Lysenkoism see Zh. Medvedev, *The Rise and Fall of T.D. Lysenko*, Princeton, 1971.
58 *Iskusstvo kino*, no. 2 (February 1948), pp.1–2.
59 L. Schwarz, 'On Modern Film Music', *Sovetskaia muzyka*, no. 3 (March 1948), p.6. Cited in Egorova, p.291.
60 Ibid.
61 T. Khrennikov, 'Muzyka v kino', *Iskusstvo kino*, no. 1 (January 1950), p.27.
62 He mentions the resolution in *Sovetskoe iskusstvo*, 14 October 1950, also promising a work glorifying 'the joyful peaceful labour of the Soviet people' – another plan that apparently came to nothing.
63 Glikman, p.247.
64 In 1967 he wrote, 'I really cannot understand why Eisenstein, and for that matter Dovzhenko, are considered such geniuses. I don't much like their work.' Having seen *October* with selections from his music he was of the opinion that 'overall my music has by and large added to it', Glikman, pp.146, 298–299.
65 Silvashko explains this and describes the film as 'completely untrue' in *1945: Brave New World*, an episode of the television series *People's Century*, BBC/WGBH, 1996.
66 Eremin, *30 Let*, p.357.
67 D. Shostakovich, 'Ne nado pugat' kompozitorov dzhazovoi "spetsifikoi"!', *Sovetskaia muzyka*, no. 11 (November 1956), p.103; *G&P*, p.183.
68 *1945: Brave New World*.
69 B. Eisenschitz (trans. T. Milne), *Nicholas Ray: an American Journey*, London, 1993, p.121. Ray also wanted Shostakovich to score *Bitter Victory* [1957] but was blocked; p.306.

70 Muradeli describes his cool relationship with Shostakovich, and the atmosphere under the Stalin personality cult, in V. Zak (trans. A.B. Ho and D. Feofanov), 'Muradeli Talks About Shostakovich', *DSCH*, no. 13 (July 2000), pp.6–10.
71 For a detailed synopsis and discussion of *The Fall of Berlin*, see R. Taylor, *Film Propaganda: Soviet Russia and Nazi Germany*, London, 1998, pp.99–122.
72 'Evidently afraid of destroying the illusion of resemblance, Shchukin passed from one statuesque pose to another in an attempt to create an uninterrupted chain of outer forms.' N. Cherkasov, *Notes of a Soviet Actor*, Moscow, n.d, p.110. Alternatively, Gelovani's could be an uncannily accurate impersonation. Speaking of Stalin in a television documentary, Vladimir Kuibyshev said: 'By his facial expression one couldn't tell if he was happy or upset or enjoying someone else's misfortune.' *Hitler and Stalin: Twin Tyrants*, Blakeway Associates, 1999.
73 Whether or not he saw the parallel, Stalin approved this distortion of reality. G. Mariamov, *Kremlevskii tzenzor: Stalin smotrit kino*, Moscow, 1992, p.110.
74 Carynnyk, p.233.
75 Interviewed in the television documentary *Stalin – The Red God*, BBC/ORF, 2001.
76 *The Oath to the People's Commissar* is sometimes cited as *Oath to Stalin*, but Derek Hulme's query to the composer was returned with the name violently crossed out.
77 F. Youens, sleevenote. XID 5225, republished in Saga EC 3366-2. In discussing the film and the symphony it is tempting to add the respective qualifying statements 'Stalinist epic' and 'the first he wrote after the death of Stalin' but the conclusions to which this might lead would be too simplistic. For more on this, see Fanning.
78 N. Khrushchev (trans. S. Talbott), *Khrushchev Remembers*, London, 1971, p.306.
79 Stalin's disappearance was not comprehensive. In 1958 *The Fall of Berlin*'s song 'Beautiful Day' was published and Sergei Vasiliev directed *In the Days of October*, in which Andro Kolabadze played Stalin. The 1987 Collected Works edition contains parts of *The Fall of Berlin* excluded from Atovmian's suite, though without the song 'Glory to Stalin', and has minimal editorial comment on the film.
80 A film student watches a monochrome clip in Márta Mészáros' autobiographical *Diary of My Loves* [Napló zerelmeimnek, Hungary, 1987].
81 Eremin, *30 Let*, p.358.
82 Kozintsev, *Complete Works*, vol. 2, p.436.
83 Eremin, *30 Let*, p.356.
84 Zorkaya, p.195.
85 One of the writers was Galina Serebriakova.
86 D. Shostakovich, 'Beseda s molodymi kompozitorami', *Sovetskaia muzyka*, no. 10 (October 1955), p.13.
87 D. Hulme, 'The Assault on the Red Hill', *DSCH*, no. 19 (Summer 2003), pp.13–14.
88 Chiaureli may also have disliked Dovzhenko. Before Beria's arrest was made public he tried to trick him into contacting the politician. G.O. Liber, *Alexander Dovzhenko: a Life in Soviet Film*, London, 2002, pp.247–248.
89 M. Turovskaya in A.Horton (ed.) *Laughter with a Lash*, Cambridge, 1993, p.76.
90 Glikman, p.299.
91 For more on Soviet cinema at the time, see Josephine Woll, *Real Images: Soviet Cinema and the Thaw*, London, 2000.

Chapter 5

1. Russian translations are *Pesnia velikikh rek* (*Song of the Great Rivers*), *Sem' rek* (*Seven Rivers*) and, used with regard to the musical fragments, *Edinstvo* (*Unity*).
2. R. Delmar, *Joris Ivens: Fifty Years of Film-Making*, London, 1979, p.107.
3. Kirsanov's verses form the climax of Shostakovich's Third Symphony (1929). Parts of the script and song texts appear in Delmar, pp.75–79.
4. P. Robeson, *Here I Stand*, Boston, 1988, pp.59–62. He learned his collaborators' names from reviews and a year later happily saw the film in Canada though it was still banned in the USA.
5. Copy in the Shostakovich family archive, and reproduced in *Collected Works 34*.
6. Letter, 26 November 1954, Bundesarchiv/Filmarchiv Berlin. Collection Joris Ivens. Schriftwechsel 4. H. Schoots, *Living Dangerously*, Amsterdam, 2000 (translated and abridged from 1995).
7. 'Censors Want Communist Film to be Cut', *Daily Telegraph*, 4 March 1955.
8. The existence of a sketch orchestrated in Atovmian's hand does not necessarily mean that Shostakovich devolved the composition work. He took a pride in doing the whole job from start to finish, even with scores in which he was not particularly interested. Atovmian was probably working on an uncompleted suite.
9. Konstantin Mardzhanov had made a version in 1928. In 1957 the Russian (though Italian-named) Antonio Spaddavecchia, perhaps inspired by the film, wrote an operatic version, and it was a TV movie in 1980.
10. Glikman, p.275.
11. A CD of transcriptions for organ (Olympia, OCD 585) has nothing to do with Shostakovich apart from including the passacaglia, and nor does a version of the 'Michelangelo Suite' for bass soloist and organ.
12. This choice was appropriate, as Voynich had an affair with the multi-personaed Sidney Reilly – the model for the television series.
13. In 1955 Shostakovich recorded a piano transcription of one item, though it was not released until 1997, perhaps because of his uncharacteristically bad playing.
14. *Sovetskaia muzyka*, no. 4, 1956.
15. I. Frolov, 'Rol' muzyki v dramaturgii fil'ma', *Iskusstvo kino*, no. 5, 1956, p.25.
16. Mussorgsky wrote a satirical song with the same title (usually translated as The Peepshow) at the expense of his musical enemies. See C. MacDonald 'The Anti-Formalist "Rayok" – Learners Start Here!' and L. Lebedinsky 'The Origin of Shostakovich's "Rayok"', *Tempo*, no. 173 (June 1990), pp.23–30, 31–32. Lebedinsky's claim of authorship is just one of the 'facts' about this piece that has since been challenged.
17. The fanfare had a more recent outing, when it heralded the arrival of a part-time Lenin impersonator at a children's party in *Comrade Boikenzhaev* [Uzbekistan, 2002].
18. Despite the dedication, the city heard it only after Kuibyshev, Moscow, London (twice) and New York. Hulme, pp.150–154.
19. The selection was by A.A Kholodiliv. For Shostakovich's attitude to Eisenstein, see Glikman, pp.146, 298–299.
20. In Yevtushenko's poem, part of *The Bratsk Hydroelectric Dam*, the hero is called Stenka Razin, but, according to Maxim, Shostakovich changed it as a mark of respect. Ho and Feofanov, p.374.

21 Shot with each side speaking its own language, where necessary the Russian version was dubbed, the German subtitled.
22 Ironically, Nagisa Oshima's film *Night and Fog in Japan* [Japan, 1960] uses Shostakovich's Fifth Symphony, and one of the characters describes him as 'the greatest socialist'.
23 Glikman, pp.90–93.
24 Ho and Feofanov, p.398.
25 Glikman, p.90.
26 *Culture and Life*, no. 1, 1961.
27 A few years earlier the artist Tuza Tarnovskaya painted *A Meeting with Rembrandt*, which shows the discovery of the painting.
28 In *Meeting on the Elbe*, his Fifth Symphony performed a similar task.
29 The opening flute solo in the Fifteenth Symphony (1971) also takes three attempts to get going.
30 Quotes from: *Sovetskaia muzyka*, no. 1, 1959; *Pravda*, 1 January 1959; *Literatura i zhizn'*, 23 January 1959; all in *G&P*, pp.199–201.
31 Glikman, pp.79, 269–271.
32 Glikman, pp.97, 99, 278.
33 Isaak Glikman, interviewed in *Cheryomushki: Another Bite of the Cherry*, a television documentary about Pimlico Opera's UK premiere; BBC Wales, 1995.
34 Gerard McBurney reorchestrated it for Pimlico Opera's fourteen-piece orchestra, and, with Jim Holmes, later revised it for Opera North's larger orchestra.
35 'Dear Shostakovich...', *BBC Music Magazine*, vol. 3, no. 8, April 1995, pp.9–10. The magazine was accompanied by a CD of extracts performed by Pimlico Opera.
36 Igor Barbashov (Moscow Operetta Theatre producer), interviewed in *Cheryomushki: Another Bite of the Cherry*.

Chapter 6

1 See M. Alekseev, *Shekspir i russkaia kul'tura*, Moscow, 1965.
2 Kozintsev refers to and discusses the poem in *Shakespeare: Time and Conscience*, (trans. J. Vining), New York, 1967, pp.165, 172.
3 Kozintsev, 'Shakespeare au cinéma', *Jeune cinéma*, nos 3–4 (December–January 1964–5), p.4.
4 Kozintsev, *Shakespeare: Time and Conscience*, p.266.
5 Kozintsev, *Shakespeare: Time and Conscience*, pp.38–45.
6 *Pravda*, 21 October 1962.
7 2 September 1963. *G&P*, pp.241–243. It appears on the four-disc set of LPs of speeches by Shostakovich, *Govorit Dmitri Shostakovich*, M40 41705–12 (record 2, side 1).
8 *Literaturnaia gazeta*, 12 October 1963.
9 Kozintsev, *Shakespeare: Time and Conscience*, p.262.
10 Glikman, p.116.
11 In a speech before the premiere. Quoted in M. Shaginian, *O Shostakoviche: stati*, Moscow, 1979, p.12.
12 Kozintsev, *Shakespeare: Time and Conscience*, p.150.
13 Around this time, the harpsichord began to be popular with Soviet avant-garde composers.

14 Kozintsev, *Shakespeare: Time and Conscience*, p.256. Despite what we hear, her dancing lesson is accompanied onscreen by a lute.
15 Kozintsev discusses pre-Raphaelite Shakespeare paintings (including this one) in *Shakespeare: Time and Conscience*, pp.17–19.
16 Volkov, pp.62–67.
17 'Spasibo za schast'e, kotoroe on mne prinosil', *Sovetskaia muzyka*, no. 9 (September 1999), pp.93–99.
18 Glikman, pp.121.
19 Glikman, pp.122.
20 The soprano describes the studio's further attempts to desexualise the story. G. Vishnevskaya, *Galina: A Russian Story*, London, 1984, pp.357–361.
21 This EMI recording dates from 1978.
22 Petr Weigl made the same decision for his version (Czechoslovakia, 1992) which in its turn, uses the Vishnevskaya recording.
23 Glikman, p.125.
24 Vishnevskaya, pp.359–361.
25 Volkov, p.81.
26 Egorova, p.290.
27 Glikman, pp.122, 289.
28 *Sovexportfilm Catalogue of Soviet Feature Films*, Moscow, n.d. (1968?), p.168.
29 Cf. Vishnevskaya, pp.357–61.
30 Oddly, when it was broadcast on British television (6 March 1969) it was credited to M. Schmidt.
31 Quoted in the London Symphony Orchestra festival programme, *Shostakovich 1906–1975*, p.66.
32 Kozintsev, *The Space of Tragedy*, p.82.
33 Kozintsev thought *Throne of Blood* [Japan, 1957] the best film version of *Macbeth*.
34 'Bydni i prazdniki muziki: interviu s Dmitriem Shostakovichem', *Izvestiia*, 7 December 1970 ['Weekday and Holiday Music: An Interview with Dmitri Shostakovich'] *G&P*, p.296.
35 Kozintsev, *The Space of Tragedy*, p.254.
36 Kozintsev, *The Space of Tragedy*, pp.204, 244.
37 Glikman, p.177.
38 As with earlier films, he seems to have written some music with no particular sequence in mind, giving them arbitrary numbers, and titling them later, once he had seen the film.
39 G. Abrahams, *Eight Soviet Composers*, Oxford, 1943, pp.29–30.
40 The notes D, E flat, C, B, when using German designation, are D, Es (=S), C, H: ['*D*mitri *SCH*ostakowitsch']. He used the motif from the Tenth Symphony on, most blatantly setting his own name to it in the satirical song 'Preface to the Complete Collection of My Works and a Brief Reflection Upon This Preface' (1966).
41 Kozintsev, *The Space of Tragedy*, p.251.
42 Glikman, p.312.
43 Transposed, it also starts the opus 87 no. 19 Fugue, but that seems less relevant.
44 In spring 1971 he set Yevtushenko's poem about her suicide, 'Yelaguba Nail'.
45 Glikman, p.311.
46 London Symphony Orchestra, p.66.

47 *Don Quixote*, Kozintsev's only major film not scored by Shostakovich, is another exploration of foolishness; Kara Karayev took his place. Shostakovich and Sollertinsky had considered a balletic version in 1935.

Legacy

1 The only film score credited to her in Macheret, *Sovetskie khudozhestvennye fil'my* is *The Girl and the Crocodile* [Devushka i krokodil, 1957]. To date she recognises only twenty-one works, and has published nothing since 1990.
2 Chant du Monde, LDC 288029/30. Film director Pavel Lungin co-wrote the libretto with the composer. The birth of the tyrannical Philip II of Spain is heralded by Shostakovich's *DSCH* motif. Karetnikov wrote a score for the film *The Legend of Thyl* [Legenda o Tile, 1976]. Though Emin Khachaturian conducted both recording and film score, there are no cast members in common and the relationship of the two projects is unclear.
3 A. Tarkovsky (trans K. Hunter-Blair), *Time Within Time*, Calcutta, 1991, pp.9, 24, 97–98.
4 M. Turovskaya, in A. Horton, pp.75–82.

Curriculum Vitae

Date	Life and Work	Historical Events
1906	9 Sept. Born in St Petersburg	
1908	8 Aug. Sister Zoya born	
1914		Outbreak of First World War. St Petersburg becomes Petrograd
1915	First piano lessons with mother	
1916	Enters Glyasser's School of Music, Petrograd. *The Soldier* (*Ode to Liberty*)	
1917	Able to play the whole of Bach's 'Well-Tempered Clavier'	Tsar Nicholas II abdicates Feb. Provisional Government 21–25 Oct. October Revolution 7 Dec. Cheka formed (forerunners of NKVD)
1918		Japan, the United States and Britain attack Siberia Apr. Russian Civil War starts Jul. All non-Party newspapers banned 11 Nov. Armistice Day

Date	Life and Work	Historical Events
1919	Passes entrance exam for Petrograd Conservatory; 'Scherzo Op. 1' (first piece he preserved)	War Communism causes shortages
1921		Famine in Russia
1922	Father dies, 'Suite for Two Pianos' (dedicated to his memory)	Lenin's first stroke
1923		USSR constitution
1924	Begins work as cinema accompanist	Petrograd becomes Leningrad after Lenin's death
1926	12 May. Premiere of 1st Symphony	
1927	Certificate of Merit at First Chopin Competition, Warsaw; 2nd Symphony ('To October')	
1928	2 Nov. US premiere of 1st Symphony *The Nose* (Nos)	First Five-Year Plan
1929	18 Mar. Premiere of *New Babylon* [Novyi Vavilon] Jul. Begins 3rd Symphony	Ukrainian kulaks liquidated
1930	Begins *Alone* [Odna] and *Lady Macbeth of Mtsensk* [Ledi Makbet Mtsenskogo uezda]	
1931	Summer–autumn. *The Golden Mountains* [Zlatye gory] and suite 10 Oct. Premiere of *Alone* 6 Nov. Premiere of *The Golden Mountains* Autumn. Premiere of *Golden Mountains* Suite	

Curriculum Vitae 131

Date	Life and Work	Historical Events
1932	13 May. Marries Nina Varzar Autumn. *The Counterplan* [Vstrechnyi] 7 Nov. Premiere of *The Counterplan* 17 Dec. Completes *Lady Macbeth of Mtsensk*	Artist's unions formed
1933	Becomes deputy of Oktyabrsky district of Leningrad; 1st Piano Concerto	Jan. Hitler becomes German Chancellor
1934	22 Jan. Premiere of *Lady Macbeth of Mtsensk; Tale of the Priest and his Worker Balda* [Skazka o pope i ego rabotnike Balda]; *Love and Hate* [Liubov' i nenavist']; *The Youth of Maxim* [Iuonst' Maksima]; *Girlfriends* [Podrugi]	18 Sept. USSR joins League of Nations 1 Dec. Sergei Kirov assassinated
1935	27 Jan. Premiere of *Youth of Maxim* 3 Mar. Premiere of *Love and Hate*	Second Five-Year Plan
1936	*Pravda* attacks *Lady Macbeth of Mtsensk* and *Limpid Stream* (Svetlyi ruchi) Premiere of *Girlfriends* 30 May. Daughter Galina born. 14 Aug. Re-release of *Golden Mountains* Forced to withdraw Fourth Symphony	21 Mar. Death of Glazunov Aug. Show trials
1937	*The Return of Maxim* [Vozvrashchenie Maksima]	Jan. 'Old Bolsheviks' purged

Date	Life and Work	Historical Events
	Volochaev Days [Volochaevskie dnie]; *The Great Citizen* (part one) [Velikii grazhdanin, 1a seriia] Teaches at Leningrad Conservatory 23 May. Premiere of *The Return of Maxim* 21 Nov. Premiere of 5th Symphony	Jun. Marshal Tukhachevsky and seven generals shot
1938	*Friends* [Druz'ia] Premiere of *Volochaev Days* 13 Feb. Premiere of The *Great Citizen* (part one) 10 May. Son Maxim born *The Man with a Gun* [Chelovek s ruzh'em] 1 Oct. Premiere of *Friends* 1 Nov. Premiere of *Man with a Gun* *The Vyborg Side* [Vyborgskaia storona]	Purges continue
1939	Completes *The Great Citizen* (part two) [Velikii grazhdanin, 2ia seriia] 2 Feb. Premiere of *Vyborg Side* Mar. Elected War Deputy to Leningrad City Council *The Story of the Silly Little Mouse* [Skazka o glupom myshonke] 27 Nov. Premiere of *The Great Citizen* (part two)	23 Aug. Stalin and Hitler sign non-aggression pact 3 Sept. Outbreak of Second World War
1940	20 May Order of the Red Banner of Labour 13 Sept. Premiere of *The Story of the Silly Little Mouse*	12 Mar. USSR signs peace treaty with Finland

Curriculum Vitae 133

Date	Life and Work	Historical Events
	Autumn *The Adventures of Korzinkina* [Prikliucheniia Korzinkinoi] 11 Nov. Premiere of *The Adventures of Korzinkina*	
1941	*Concert Waltz* [Kontsert val's] Illness prevents him joining the People's Volunteer Corps 1 Oct. Evacuated to Kuibyshev Stalin Prize for Piano Quintet	22 Jun. Germany invades USSR 30 Aug. Start of siege of Leningrad
1942	Stalin Prize for 7th Symphony Honoured Artist of the RSFSR	12 Sept. Start of Battle of Stalingrad
1943	Professor of Composition in Moscow Honorary Member of the American Institute of Art and Literature Begins *Zoya* [Zoia]	7 Feb. End of Battle of Stalingrad
1944	11 Feb. Death of Ivan Sollertinsky – 2nd Piano Trio (dedicated to him) 22 Nov. Premiere of *Zoya*	26 Jan. End of Siege of Leningrad
1945	9th Symphony *Simple People* [Prostye liudi]	2 May Berlin surrenders to Soviet troops
1946	*Simple People* withdrawn Order of Lenin Stalin Prize for 2nd Piano Trio	United Nations takes over from League of Nations
1947	9 Feb. Deputy of the Supreme Soviet RSFSR	

Date	Life and Work	Historical Events
	April–Autumn *The Young Guard* [Molodaia gvardiia] 16 Dec. Premiere of *Pirogov*	
1948	People's Artist of the RSFSR 10 Feb. Central Committee attacks composers including Shostakovich. Many of his works are banned. *Michurin* and *Meeting on the Elbe* [Vstrecha na El'be] 11 Oct. Premiere of *The Young Guard* (part one) 25 Nov. Premiere of *The Young Guard* (part two)	31 Aug. Death of Andrei Zhdanov Ilya Trauberg dies
1949	1 Jan. Premiere of *Michurin* 16 Mar. Premiere of *Meeting on the Elbe* 25–28 Mar. Forced to go to New York for Congress of Peace *The Fall of Berlin* [Padenie Berlina] and Suite	Autumn. Official anti-Semitism becomes overt
1950	21 Jan. Premiere of *Fall of Berlin* 10 Jun. Premiere of *Fall of Berlin* Suite. *Belinsky.* Stalin Prize for *Song of the Forests*	
1951	*Young Guard* Suite *The Unforgettable Year 1919* [Nezabyvaemyi 1919-i god] and Suite	
1952	3 May. Premiere of *The Unforgettable Year 1919* Suite *The Sun Shines Over the Motherland* and 5th String	Stalin prepares for a new wave of purges

Curriculum Vitae 135

Date	Life and Work	Historical Events
	Quartet. Stalin Prize for Ten Poems on Texts by Revolutionary Poets	
1953	Premieres of suites from *Belinsky* and *The Young Guard* 10th Symphony	Jan. 'Doctors' plot' 5 Mar. Deaths of Stalin and Prokofiev Jul. Khrushchev wins power struggle Dec. Beria executed
1954	27 Mar. People's Artist of the USSR Spring. *Hamlet* [Gamlet] (theatre score) 4 Sep. International Peace Prize *The Song of the Rivers* [Das Lied der Ströme] Nov. Premiere of *The Song of the Rivers* 4 Dec. Wife Nina dies 9 Dec. Honoured by Swedish Royal Musical Academy	Security services reformed as KGB Beginning of 'virgin lands' scheme
1955	*The Gadfly* [Ovod] and suite 12 Apr. Premiere of *The Gadfly* 9 Nov. Mother dies	Beginning of 'the Thaw'
1956	Finishes *The First Echelon* [Pervyi eshelon] 15 Jan. Diploma of St Cecilia, Rome 29 Apr. Premiere of *The First Echelon* 25 Aug. Premiere of *Simple People* [1945] Marries Margarita Kainova 25 Sept. Lenin Prize on 50th birthday	14–25 Feb. 20th Party Congress; Khrushchev denounces Stalin's personality cult Oct.–Nov. Hungarian uprising

Date	Life and Work	Historical Events
1957	Becomes Secretary of the Union of Soviet Composers (post held until 1975) 2nd Piano Concerto and 11th Symphony	Khrushchev continues to remove opponents First tower block (e.g. Cheremushki)
1958	Mar. Begins orchestrating Mussorgsky's *Khovanshchina* 22 Apr. Lenin Prize for 11th Symphony 28 May 1948 Decree rescinded May. French Commander Order of Art and Literature 25 Jun. Honorary doctorate from Oxford University Sept.–Nov. Treated for weakness in right arm. *Cheremushki* 9 Oct. Sibelius Prize	
1959	24 Jan. Stage premiere of *Cheremushki* 26 Apr. Finishes *Khovanshchina* Divorces Margarita Kainova Honoured by American Academy of Sciences and Mexico Conservatory	Sept. Khrushchev visits United States; beginning of détente Beginning of Sino-Soviet conflict
1960	Feb. Treatment for right hand 9 Apr. Becomes First Secretary of Union of Composers of the RSFSR Jul.–Aug. *Five Days, Five Nights* [Piat' dnei, piat' nochei] *Belinsky* Suite Oct. Breaks leg	
1961	*Five Days, Five Nights* Suite and *Fragments from the Maxim Trilogy*	12 Apr. Yuri Gagarin sings Shostakovich's song 'The Motherland Hears' (Rodina slyshit) in space

Curriculum Vitae 137

Date	Life and Work	Historical Events
	Sept. Accepted as full member of Communist Party 23 Nov. Premiere of *Five Days, Five Nights* 30 Dec. Premiere of 4th Symphony	13 Aug. Berlin Wall construction started Oct. Stalin removed from Lenin mausoleum
1962	7 Jan. Premiere of *Five Days, Five Nights* Suite Mar.–Jul. 13th Symphony Jun. More treatment for right hand Aug. Visits Edinburgh Festival; 22 of his pieces played Nov. Marries Irina Supinskaya 30 Dec. Premiere of *Cheremushki* (film) Delegate of Supreme Soviet	Oct. Cuban missile crisis
1963	Honorary member of UNESCO International Music Committee *Michurin* Suite Begins *Hamlet* [Gamlet]	Crop failure; wheat bought from Canada
1964	Finishes *Hamlet* 15–23 Feb. Gorky Festival dedicated to his music. 24 Apr. Premiere of *Hamlet* *Hamlet* Suite, 9th and 10th String Quartets and *The Execution of Stepan Razin*	12 Oct. Fall of Khrushchev; Brezhnev takes over
1965	Jan. Moscow neurological hospital Jun. *A Year is Like a Lifetime* [God kak zhizn'] Nov. Honoured by Serbian Academy of Art	

Date	Life and Work	Historical Events
1966	2 Mar. 'Preface to the Complete Collection of My Works and a Brief Reflection Upon This Preface' 20 Apr. Severe respiratory problems; Crimean sanatorium 28 May Heart attack Aug. Royal Philharmonic Gold Medal 25 Sept. Premiere of *Katerina Izmailova* film 5 Oct. Order of Lenin Hero of Socialist Labour	De-Stalinisation halted; trial of Daniel and Sinyavsky
1967	15 Mar. Honoured by Austrian Republic Summer. *October* (symphonic poem) Sept. Breaks right leg in car accident *Sofia Perovskaia*	
1968	Jan. Premiere of *Sofia Perovskaia* 12th String Quartet Honoured by Bavarian Academy of Fine Arts 5 Nov. Glinka State Prize for *The Execution of Stepan Razin* International Committee in Defence of Peace member	Jan. Prague Spring 20–21 Aug. Invasion of Czechoslovakia Red Square protesters tried
1969	14th Symphony 1–23 Aug. Sanatorium at Lake Baikal *A Year is Like a Lifetime* Suite	
1970	Feb. Mozart Society of Vienna medal Apr.–Jun. *King Lear* [Korol' lir]	Large-scale Jewish emigration

Date	Life and Work	Historical Events
	10 Aug. Completes 13th String Quartet 10 Nov. First Prize at All-Union Literature and Art Contest for *March of the Soviet Militia* Honorary member of Society of Finnish Composers About half the year spent in Kurgan Hospital	
1971	4 Feb. Premiere of *King Lear* Jun.–Jul. 15th Symphony 17 Sept. Second heart attack Mikhail Shapiro dies Order of the October Revolution	11 Sept. Death of Khrushchev
1972	Golden Order 'Friends of the People' (GDR); Golden Lira (Italy); Doctor of Music, University College of Dublin 26 Jun. Nikolai Rabinovich dies	New wave of censorship Repression in Ukraine and Lithuania
1973	Honoured by Northwestern University, Evanstone, USA, and in Denmark Mar.–Apr. 14th String Quartet Jul.–Aug. Six Songs on Poems by Marina Tsvetaeva 6 Oct. Death of sister Maria Grigori Kozintsev dies	
1974	Spring. 15th String Quartet 'Suite on Verses by Michelangelo' Glinka State Prize for *Loyalty* and 14th String Quartet	8 Aug. President Nixon resigns (United States) 13 Dec. Solzhenitsyn expelled from USSR
1975	Honoured by French Academy of Fine Arts	

Date	Life and Work	Historical Events
	Apr.–Jul. Viola Sonata 3 Aug. Hospitalised for last time. 9 Aug. Shostakovich dies at 6.30 p.m. in Moscow 14 Aug. Buried in Novodevichyi Cemetery, Moscow	
1981	Documentary *Viola Sonata* (Sokurov) banned	

Filmography

Details of the films for which Shostakovich wrote original scores, in chronological order of release, apart from the delayed *Simple People*. Soundtrack performers are excluded for restorations with new soundtracks. Where not credited, suites and arrangements were compiled by the composer. Publication details include the old Collected Works edition, cited as CW followed by the volume number, usually 34 (choral pieces and songs) and 41 or 42 (orchestral pieces). The New Collected Works (NCW) will include more extensive selections from more film scores.

The recordings list concentrates on CDs, though some older recording are included but catalogue numbers are omitted. For fuller details, see Hulme. As a brief guide, the conductors who have recorded several scores and the labels on which they appear are: Chailly (Decca); Jurowski (Capriccio); Mnatsakanov (Russian Disc – now defunct – and Citadel); Rozhdestvensky (Olympia and BMG Melodiya); Serebrier (RCA); Maxim Shostakovich (Melodiya LP, Melodiya CD, BMG and Collins); and Sinaisky (Chandos).

New Babylon [Novyi Vavilon] B/w. 85 minutes. Premiere 18 March 1929, simultaneously in the Piccadilly and Giant cinemas, Leningrad. Modern accompanied premiere (18 frames per second). Paris 1975. Ars Nova Ensemble/Marius Constant. British accompanied premiere (varying speed). 22 September 1982. Queen Elizabeth Hall. London Lyric Orchestra/Omri Hadari. Broadcast BBC2, 11 January 1986.
Dirs/Scen: Grigori Kozintsev and Leonid Trauberg
Music: Opus 18. *Complete*: Sikorski. *Suite*: Rozhdestvensky (50 minutes). Sovetskii kompozitor, 1976.
Recordings: *Complete*: Judd (Capriccio). *Suite*: Rozhdestvensky (Russian Disc), Polyansky (Chandos).

Alone [Odna] B/w with colour sequence. 81 minutes. Sixth reel lost (music still exists). Premiere 10 October 1931, Splendid Palace, Leningrad.
Dirs/Scen: Grigori Kozintsev and Leonid Trauberg
Sound: Lev Arnshtam and Ilia Volk
Music: Opus 26. Soundtrack conductor Nikolai Rabinovich. *Suites*: Rozhdestvensky (12 mins); McBurney; Smirnov (2000). Extensive but incomplete fragments in CW41. Full score to be published as NCW106.
Recordings: *CW41*: Jurowski (Capriccio). *CW41 without soloists*: Mnatsakanov (Russian Disc). *Rozhdestvensky Suite*: Rozhdestvensky (BMG). *Selections*: Chailly (Decca), Sinaisky (Chandos).

The Golden Mountains [Zlatye gory] B/w. 131 minutes. Revision 90 minutes. Premiere 6 November 1931, Artistic Cinema, Leningrad. Revision, 14 August 1936.
Dir: Sergei Yutkevich
Scen: Andrei Mikhailovsky, Vladimir Nedobrovo, Yutkevich, Lev Arnshtam and Alexei Chapigin
Sound: Arnshtam, Ilia Volk
Music: Opus 30. Conductor Nikolai Rabinovich. Suite (23 minutes), 1931. Suite: CW41.
Recordings *Suite:* Rozhdestvensky (BMG and Russian Disc), Serebrier (RCA), Mnatsakanov (Citadel).

The Counterplan [Vstrechnyi] B/w. 115 minutes. Premiere 7 November 1932, Leningrad.
Dirs: Sergei Yutkevich and Fridrikh Ermler
Scen: Lev Arnshtam, D. Del, Yutkevich and Ermler
Sound: Ilia Volk and D. Dmitriev
Music: Opus 33. Conductor Nikolai Rabinovich. Selections: CW34 and CW41.
Recordings: *Fragments*: Mnatsakanov (Russian Disc), Chailly (Decca).

The Tale of the Priest and His Worker Balda [Skazka o pope i ego rabotnike Balde] B/w. Incomplete. All but 60 metres destroyed in war.
Dir: Mikhail Tsekhanovsky
Music: Opus 36. Written from 3 March 1933 to 1935. Aleksandr Melik-Pashaev conducted a suite in 1935. Khentova's opera: Sovetskii kompozitor, 1981
Recordings: *Suite*: Rozhdestvensky (BMG). *Selections from Khentova's opera*: Kozhin (Boheme).

The Youth of Maxim [Iunost' Maksima] B/w. 98 minutes. Premiere 27 January 1935. Moscow.
Dirs/Scen: Grigori Kozintsev and Leonid Trauberg
Sound: Ilia Volk (Assistants B Litkin and P Artemeva)
Sound editor: A. Ruzanova
Music: Opus 41a. Conductor Nikolai Rabinovich. Accordionist M. Makarov. Prologue CW41.
Recordings: Jurowski (Capriccio). See also *The Vyborg Side* [1939].

Love and Hate [Liubov' i nenavist'] B/w. 80 minutes. Premiere 3 March 1935.
Dir: Albert Gendelshtein
Scen: Sergei Ermolinsky and Vasili Pronin

Sound: A. Gornshtein and D. Blok
Music: Opus 38. None published.
Recordings: None.

Girlfriends [Podrugi] B/w. 93 minutes. Premiere 19 February 1936.
Dir: Lev Arnshtam
Scen: Arnshtam and Raia Vasilieva
Sound: I. Dmitriev and Ilia Volk
Music: Opus 41b. None published.
Recordings: *Selections*: Postnikova et al. (Melodiya LP).

The Return of Maxim [Vozvrashchenie Maksima] B/w. 100 minutes. Premiere 23 May 1937.
Dirs/Scen: Grigori Kozintsev and Leonid Trauberg
Sound: Ilia Volk and G. Khutoriansky
Music: Opus 45. Conductor Nikolai Rabinovich: Waltz Sovetskii kompozitor, 1959.
Recordings: See *The Vyborg Side* [1939].

Volochaev Days [Volochaevskie dni] B/w. 112 minutes. Premiere 20 January 1938.
Dirs/Scen: Georgi and Sergei Vasiliev
Sound: A. Bekker
Music: Opus 48. Conductor Nikolai Rabinovich. Selections CW34 and CW41.
Recordings: Sinaisky (Chandos).

The Great Citizen (part one) [Velikii grazhdanin, seriia 1] B/w. 111 minutes. Premiere 13 February 1938.
Dir: Fridrikh Ermler
Scen: Mikhail Bleiman, Mikhail Bolshintsov and Ermler
Sound: I. Dmitriev, Assistant G. Elbert
Music: Opus 52. None published.
Recordings: None.

Friends [Druz'ia] B/w. 111 minutes. Premiere 1 October 1938.
Dir: Lev Arnshtam
Scen: Arnshtam and N. Tikhonov
Sound: N Bukatov
Music: Opus 51. Vocalise: CW34.
Recordings: None.

The Man with a Gun [Chelovek s ruzh'em] B/w. 100 minutes. Premiere 1 November 1938.
Dir: Sergei Yutkevich
Scen: Nikolai Pogodin, from his play *November*
Sound: K. Gordon
Music: Opus 53. Five items, all in CW41.
Recordings: Mnatsakanov (Russian Disc), Sinaisky (Chandos).

The Vyborg Side [Vyborgskaia storona] B/w. 111 minutes. Premiere 2 February 1939.
Dir/Scen: Grigori Kozintsev and Leonid Trauberg

Sound: Ilia Volk and B. Khutoriansky
Music: Opus 50. Conductor Nikolai Rabinovich. Excerpts from 'the music to the *Maxim* trilogy', Sovetskii kompozitor, 1951. Overture only: CW41.
Recordings: *Excerpts from the music to the Maxim trilogy*: Jurowski (Capriccio), Mnatsakanov (Citadel), Sinaisky (Chandos) *Overture*: Mnatsakanov (Russian Disc).

The Great Citizen (part two) [Velikii grazhdanin, seriia 2] B/w. 120 minutes. Premiere 27 November 1939.
Dir: Fridrikh Ermler
Scen: Mikhail Bleiman, Mikhail Bolshintsov and Ermler
Sound: I. Dmitriev
Music: Opus 55. Funeral March: CW41.
Recordings: *Funeral March*: Mnatsakanov (Russian Disc), Chailly (Decca).

The Story of the Silly Little Mouse [Skazka o glupom myshonke] Colour. 15 minutes. Premiere 13 September 1940.
Dir/Scen: Mikhail Tsekhanovsky
Sound: A. Bekker. Sound editor V. Nazarenko
Music: Opus 56. Boris Tiles' arrangement: CW41 and *DSCH* Publishers.
Recordings: Mnatsakanov (Citadel), Tiles (Boheme). *Orchestral version*: Chailly (Decca).

The Adventures of Korzinkina [Prikliucheniia Korzinkinoi] B/w. 38 minutes. Premiere 11 November 1940.
Dir: Klement Mintz
Scen: Mintz and Grigori Iagdfeld
Sound: Z. Zalkind and E. Nesterov
Music: Opus 59. Suite: Rozhdestvensky (10 minutes) CW41.
Recordings: Rozhdestvensky (Olympia and BMG – same recording).

Zoya [Zoia] B/w. 85 minutes. Premiere 22 September 1944.
Dir: Lev Arnshtam
Scen: Arnshtam and Boris Chirskov
Music: Opus 64. Suite Atovmian (32 minutes). Selections from score: CW34 and CW41.
Recordings: *Suite*: Maxim Shostakovich (BMG), Jurowski (Capriccio), Mnatsakanov (Russian Disc).

Simple People [Prostye liudi] B/w. 78 minutes. Premiere 25 August 1956.
Dir/Scen: Grigori Kozintsev and Leonid Trauberg
Sound: Ilia Volk
Music: Written in 1945. Opus 71. None published.
Recordings: None.

Pirogov B/w. 92 minutes. Premiere 16 December 1947.
Dir: Grigori Kozintsev
Scen: Yuri German
Sound: Ilia Volk and B. Khutoriansky
Music: Opus 76. Suite: Atovmian, 1951 (17 minutes). Waltz: Sovetskii kompozitor.

Recordings: *Suite*: Maxim Shostakovich (BMG), Serebrier (RCA), Mnatsakanov (Citadel). *Fragments*: Chailly (Decca).

The Young Guard [Molodaia gvardiia] B/w. Part one: 101 minutes. Part two: 86 minutes. Premiere: seven scenes shown on 29 June 1946 during VGIK exams. Part one – 11 October 1948. Part two – 25 October 1948.
Dir: Sergei Gerasimov
Scen: Gerasimov and Alexander Fadeyev
Sound: N. Pisarev
Music: Opus 75. Initial sketches Moscow, 25 April 1947. Bulk of the score between summer 1947 and March 1948. USSR Ministry of Cinematography Symphony Orchestra/A. Roitman. Suite: Atovmian, 1951 (22 minutes). Muzgiz, 1950. Premiered 1953, Moscow. Moscow Radio Symphony Orchestra/Alexander Gauk. Overture: CW42.
Recordings: Gamburg (Olympia), Mnatsakanov (Russian Disc).

Michurin Colour. 101 minutes. Premiere 1 January 1949.
Dir/Scen: Alexander Dovzhenko
Sound: N. Timartsev
Music: Opus 78. Suite: Atovmian, 1964 (30 minutes). Selections: CW41 and CW42.
Recordings: Maxim Shostakovich (Melodiya CD), Serebrier (RCA).

Meeting on the Elbe [Vstrecha na Elb'e] B/w. 106 minutes. Premiere 16 March 1949.
Dir: Grigori Alexandrov
Scen: Tur brothers and Lev Sheinin
Sound: S. Minervin
Music: Opus 80. Suite, 1948 (?). Selections: CW34 and CW42.
Recordings: *Songs*: Paul Robeson (Melodiya LP); Ernst Busch (one on Melodiya LP; one on Aurora LP).

The Fall of Berlin [Padenie Berlina] Sovcolour. 150 minutes. Premiere 21 January 1950. Germany – part one: 23 June 1950. Part two: 7 July 1950.
Dir: Mikhail Chiaureli
Scen: Chiaureli and Piotr Pavlenko
Sound: B. Volsky
Music: Opus 82. All-Union Radio Orchestra and Choir/Alexander Gauk. Suite: Atovmian, 1950 (22 minutes). Muzgiz, 1952. Premiered 10 June 1950, Moscow, same forces as score. Selections: CW34 and CW42.
Recordings: *Suite*: Jurowski (Capriccio), Serebrier (RCA). *Complete music*: Adriano (Marco Polo).

The Unforgettable Year 1919 [Nezabyvaemyi 1919-i god] Colour. 108 minutes. Premiere 3 May 1952.
Dir: Mikhail Chiaureli
Scen: Chiaureli, Vsevolod Vishnevsky and Aleksandr Filimonov
Sound: B. Volsky
Music: Opus 89. Suite: Muzgiz, 1955.
Recordings: *Fragments*: Gauk (Monitor LP), Maksimiuk (HMV). *Complete suite*: Adriano (Marco Polo).

Belinsky [Belinskii] B/w. 96 minutes. Premiere 4 June 1953.
Dir: Grigori Kozintsev
Scen: Yuri German, Galina Serebrovskaia and Kozintsev
Sound: Ilia Volk
Music: Opus 85. Orchestra and Chorus of the Leningrad Radio-Committee/Nikolai Rabinovich. Suite: Atovmian, 1960 (30 minutes). Sovetskii kompozitor, 1960. Four choruses: CW34.
Recordings: *Suite*: Mnatsakanov (Citadel).

The Song of the Rivers [Das Lied der Ströme aka Pesnia Velikikh Rek] B/w. 92 minutes. Premiere 17 September 1954, Berlin.
Dir: Joris Ivens
Scen: Ivens and Vladimir Pozner
Sound: Heinz Reusch
Song texts: Bertolt Brecht translated by Semion Kirsanov
Music: Opus 95. Leipzig Radio Orchestra and Chorus/Walter Raatzke. CW34 and CW42.
Recordings: *Fragments*: Genova and Dimitrov Piano Duet (CPO), Orbelian (Delos).

The Gadfly [Ovod] Sovcolour. 94 minutes. Premiere 12 April 1955.
Dir: Alexander Faintsimmer
Scen: Evgeni Gabrilovich
Sound: Ilia Volk
Music: Opus 97. Suite: Atovmian, 1955 (40 minutes). Muzgiz, 1960. 19 pieces in original orchestration, CW42.
Recordings: *Suite*: Emin Khachaturian (HMV). *Fragments (original orchestration)*: Chailly (Decca).

The First Echelon [Pervyi eshelon] Colour. 114 minutes. Premiere 29 April 1956.
Dir: Mikhail Kalatozov
Scen: Kalatozov and Nikolai Pogodin
Sound: V. Popov
Music: Opus 99. Suite: 1956 (?) (40 minutes). Suite: Sovetskii kompozitor, 1962. Two songs, CW34.
Recordings: *Fragment*: Altshuler (Manchester).

Khovanshchina Sovcolour. 135 minutes. Premiere *Film* 23 May 1959, Leningrad. *Stage* 25 November 1960, Kirov Theatre, Leningrad.
Dir: Vera Stroeva
Scen: Anna Abramova, Stroeva and Shostakovich
Sound: V. Zorin
Music: Opus 106. Moscow, summer 1958.
Recordings: Abbado (DG).

Five Days, Five Nights [Piat' dnei, piat' nochei] B/w. 103 minutes. Premiere 23 November 1961, Moscow.
Dir: Lev Arnshtam
Scen: Arnshtam and Wolfgang Ebeling
Sound: Bernd Gerwein and Boris Volsky

Music: Opus 111. Moscow and Dresden, August 1960 and early 1961. State Cinematography Orchestra in Moscow. Suite: Atovmian, 1961 (25 minutes). Muzyka, 1970. Premiere 7 January 1962, USSR Cinematograph Orchestra/ Emin Khachaturian (Moscow radio). One item, CW42.
Recordings: *Selections*: Emin Khachaturian (MK LP), Serebrier (RCA), Freeman (Class). *Suite*: Judd (Capriccio).

Cheremushki Colour. 85 minutes. Premiere *Stage* 24 January 1959, Moscow Operetta Theatre. *Film* 30 December 1962.
Dir: Gerbert Rappaport
Scen: Vladimir Mass and Mikhail Chervinsky
Sound: G. Elbert
Music: Opus 105. Stage version: Written, autumn 1957 and September and November 1958. Film revisions: 1962. CW24 and CW25. Leningrad Philharmonic/Nikolai Rabinovich.
Recordings: *Complete*: Rozhdestvensky (Chandos). *Almost complete*: Stoliarov (Melodiya LP). *Abbreviated in English*: Kani (BBC Music Magazine). *Excerpts*: Kostelanetz (Sony), Chailly (Decca).

Hamlet [Gamlet] B/w. 150 minutes. Premiere 19 April 1964, Moscow.
Dir/scen: Grigori Kozintsev
Sound: B. Khutoriansky
Music: Opus 116. Leningrad Philharmonic/Nikolai Rabinovich. Suite: Atovmian, 1964 (30 minutes). Muzyka 1968. 15 items in CW42.
Recordings: Rabinovich (Melodiya LP), Serebrier (RCA), Grin (Capriccio). *Fragments*: Herrmann (Decca), Freeman (Class), Chailly (Decca). *Complete published music*: Yablonsky (Naxos).

A Year is Like a Lifetime [God kak zhizn']. Colour. 147 minutes. Premiere press show, 18 March 1965 Moscow, and opened in the Rossiia Cinema on 24 March 1965.
Dir: Grigori Roshal
Scen: Roshal and Galina Serebriakova
Sound: I. Shpinel
Music: Opus 120. Suite: Atovmian, 1969 (27 minutes). Sovetskii kompozitor, 1970.
Recordings: Maxim Shostakovich (Melodiya LP).

Katerina Izmailova Sovcolour. 116 minutes. Premiere stage: 25 December 1962. Film: 25 September 1966.
Dir: Mikhail Shapiro
Scen: Shostakovich and Shapiro
Sound: Ilia Volk
Sound editor: A. Tubenshiak
Music: Opus 114. Revised from *Lady Macbeth of Mtsensk* (opus 29) 1956 to 31 January 1963. Sometimes designated opus 29/114. Sevchenko Opera and Ballet Company of Kiev/Konstantin Simeonov. CW20 to CW22.
Recordings: Turchak (Chant du Monde).

Sofia Perovskaia Colour. 107 minutes. Premiere 6 May 1968.
Dir: Lev Arnshtam

Scen: Yevgeny Gabrilovich and Arnshtam
Sound: S. Bengerovsky and S. Valiushok
Music: Opus 132. Unidentified orchestra/I Roitman. 16 items in CW42.
Recordings: Mnatsakanov (Russian Disc). *Waltz*: Chailly (Decca).

King Lear [Korol' Lir] B/w. 137 minutes. Premiere 4 February 1971.
Dir/Scen: Grigori Kozintsev
Sound: Edward Vanunts
Music: Opus137. Leningrad Philharmonic, conductors Dzhemal-Eddin Dalgat and Nikolai Rabinovich. 'People's Lament' CW34. 20 items in CW42.
Recordings: *Selections*: Serebrier (RCA), Jurowski (Capriccio), Sinaisky (Chandos).

Further Reading

Shostakovich

DSCH Journal. The two series contain invaluable background materials on Shostakovich's life and works. Cited as *DSCH* [Roman numeral] or *DSCH* [no.].

O. Dvornichenko, *Shostakovich*, DVD-ROM CHAN 55001, Chandos, 2000. Includes documents, photographs, a work list, discography and film clips, including the surviving fragment of *The Tale of the Priest*. The CD-ROM has slightly less material.

L. Fay, *Shostakovich: A Life*, Oxford, 2000. A generally reliable, if dry, guide to most of the events in Shostakovich's life. The cinema work is largely overlooked.

I.D. Glikman (trans. A. Phillips), *Story of a Friendship: the Letters of Dmitry Shostakovich to Isaak Glikman with a Commentary by Isaak Glikman*, London, 2001. From *Pis'ma k drugu: Dmitry Shostakovich Isaaku Glikmanu*, Moscow and St Petersburg, 1993.

L.G. Grigoriev [alias Ginzburg] and Ya.M. Platek (comps.) (trans. A. and N. Roxburgh), *Dmitry Shostakovich: About His Life and His Times*, Moscow, 1981. From M.M. Yakovlev, *D. Shostakovich o vremeni i o sebe, 1926–1975*, Moscow, 1980. A collection of Shostakovich's writings, broadcasts and interviews. NB: The English and Russian pagination is different. Cited as *G&P*.

D. Hulme, *Dmitri Shostakovich: a Catalogue, Bibliography and Discography*, Lanham, 2002. The standard (and indispensable) guide of its type.

B. Schwartz, *Music and Musical Life in Soviet Russia, 1917–1981*, Bloomington, 1983.

D. Shostakovich, *Collected Works*, Moscow, 1979–1987. In forty-two volumes, the last two contain extracts from some previously unpublished film scores, and volume 34 contains some songs and choral pieces from films. The new 150-volume *Collected Works* (Moscow, 1999–) will include complete scores of the films.

E. Wilson, *Shostakovich: A Life Remembered*, London, 1994. Interviews with, and articles by, friends of Shostakovich.

Soviet Cinema

P. Babitsky and J. Rimberg, *The Soviet Film Industry*, New York, 1955.
P. Kenez, *Cinema and Soviet Society from the Revolution to the Death of Stalin*, London, 2001.
J. Leyda, *Kino: A History of Russian and Soviet Film*, London, 1983.
R. Taylor (co-ed. and trans.) and I. Christie (co-ed.), *The Film Factory: Russian and Soviet Cinema in Documents 1896–1939*, London, 1988. Cited as *FF*.
J. Woll, *Real Images: Soviet Cinema and the Thaw*, London, 2000.

Soviet Film Music

T. Egorova (trans. T.A. Ganf and N.A. Egonova), *Soviet Film Music: An Historical Survey*, Amsterdam, 1997.